THE
CAPTAIN'S
CHALLENGE

THE
CAPTAIN'S
CHALLENGE

WINNING
THE RYDER CUP

BRUCE CRITCHLEY

ICON BOOKS

Published in the UK in 2008 by
Icon Books Ltd, The Old Dairy,
Brook Road, Thriplow,
Cambridge SG8 7RG
email: info@iconbooks.co.uk
www.iconbooks.co.uk

Sold in the UK, Europe, South Africa and Asia
by Faber & Faber Ltd, 3 Queen Square,
London WC1N 3AU or their agents

Distributed in the UK, Europe, South Africa and Asia
by TBS Ltd, TBS Distribution Centre, Colchester Road
Frating Green, Colchester CO7 7DW

This edition published in Australia in 2008
by Allen & Unwin Pty Ltd,
PO Box 8500, 83 Alexander Street,
Crows Nest, NSW 2065

Distributed in Canada by
Penguin Books Canada,
90 Eglinton Avenue East, Suite 700,
Toronto, Ontario M4P 2YE

ISBN: 978-184831-021-6

Typesetting and design by Simmons Pugh

Printed and bound in the UK by Cromwell Press

CONTENTS

FOREWORD

Tournament golf is what I do. I feel so lucky to have had such a successful career doing something I enjoy so much. Competitive golf has been the driving force of my life for so many years and I am grateful that for over twenty of them I have been able to compete at the highest level and come out on top often enough to have made the journey wonderfully worthwhile.

In the midst all this is the Ryder Cup. In many ways it is the opposite of everything we do during the 23 months between each epic encounter. We get together as a band of brothers; we play with and for each other. We play foursomes, we play fourballs and, of course, it is matchplay.

It may only be one week every two years, and you may be able to forget it in the odd years in between, but from the time the gun goes for the start of qualification for the side, that week the following September is rarely far from your thoughts.

I feel privileged to have been part of the Ryder Cup odyssey for much of my professional life. I did not play in the 1980s when Tony Jacklin laid the foundations for the great contests that have ensued, but have played under every captain since. Each one has brought different qualities to the job, has done the job differently, and, in every instance, has had a huge part to play in the many successes and few failures that have been the

Ryder Cup saga while I have been part of it.

I came to the side while those great players – those major championship winners from the 1980s – were still at their peak. They had been the engine room of the Jacklin years, the foundation on which he built teams to compete with and defeat the Americans; to put aside the drear half-century of defeat that had gone before.

When I first started playing the big worry was: would we still be able to win once these giants had passed on? We lost the first two matches I played in – narrowly, but still we lost. By the time we got to Oak Hill in 1995 the winning points, the building blocks of victory, were going to have to come from somewhere else. That year, gloriously, they did.

Obviously I have scrapbooks full of Ryder Cup memories and hopefully more still to come on the playing front. I would, of course, be delighted if one day I was invited to undertake the role of European Cup captain. Should that day come, I will draw on the memories and inspiration of those who went before and under whom I played. It will be a great help to have this book on hand to fill in any of the gaps left behind by the passage of time.

Colin Montgomerie

Perthshire, 2008

CHAPTER ONE

The Barren Years

History

Prior to the first true match for the Ryder Cup in 1927, there had been a couple of unofficial meetings between Great Britain and America. The first took place in 1921 at Gleneagles around the time of The Open Championship, played that year across the hills at St Andrews. It was mostly a social affair, but they kept the score and the home side won by 10½ points to 4½. A similar informal gathering took place five years later over the East Course at Wentworth, again with 'our' team coming out well on top, indeed the Americans only winning one match.

Encouraged by the obvious enjoyment of both sides for the contest and the goodwill it seemed to engender, Samuel Ryder, a keen golfer from Verulam in Hertfordshire, presented the trophy that bears his name for a biennial competition between the two nations. Abe Mitchell was the professional at Verulam and along with George Duncan, one of the best players of the day. He was also Sam Ryder's coach and it is Mitchell's image that sits atop the trophy.

The first official outing for the Ryder Cup took place the following year in Worcester, Massachusetts. This one set the pattern for decades to come, particularly when in America. Great Britain won one match out of four in the foursomes and just 1½ from eight in the singles. The scoreline reflects just how overwhelmed the visitors were by America, many of whom were going there for the first time.

'The whole thing about going to America was a culture shock for most of us,' Arthur Havers, the 1923 Open Champion said afterwards. 'When we got to New York, the entire team and officials were whisked through without bothering with customs and immigration formalities.

'There was a fleet of limousines waiting for us at the dockside, and, with police outriders flanking us with their sirens at full blast, we sped through New York. Traffic was halted to let us through; it was a whole new world for us. Everywhere we went we were overwhelmed by the hospitality and kindness of the Americans.

'Suddenly we were in a world of luxury and plenty, so different from home. It was something we had never expected. Even the clubhouses were luxurious with deep pile carpets, not like the often rundown and shabby clubhouses at home, which was all most of us really knew.'

Tee to green there wasn't much to separate the two sides, but on and around the putting surfaces it was a different story. Even back then, greens were vastly superior in America to anything we had in Britain. The

Americans expected to hole out regularly from 20 or 30 feet, while our professionals were used to just trying to get down in two from that sort of range.

Home advantage was made to count in 1929 when the match was played at Moortown in Leeds. The Americans led by a point after the foursomes, but once again, shown the way by an outstanding captain's innings from George Duncan – who beat his opposite number Walter Hagan 10/8 – Great Britain came back to win the singles 5½–2½ and the overall match by 7 matches to 5. Duncan's natural successor as Britain's leading player, Henry Cotton, played his first Ryder Cup that year and won his singles against Al Watrous.

With the visitors again finding it difficult to adjust after the long sea voyage and with little time to settle on arrival, it was another one-sided affair when we went back there in 1931. The match was at Scioto Country Club in Ohio, not far from where Jack Nicklaus would build Muirfield Village some 50 years later. George Duncan was no longer such a force and Great Britain managed only 3 points out of the 12, again befuddled by conditions alien to our way of playing.

One of our great links courses, Southport and Ainsdale, played host in 1933 and old newsreels of the day show how quickly this head-to-head team contest had caught the public's imagination. It was Henry Longhurst's first Ryder Cup too.

There were thousands of people who rushed about the course, herded, not always successfully, by volunteer stewards brandishing long bamboo poles with pennants at the end, which earned them the name of the 'Southport Lancers'. Many had come to see the golf, more perhaps to see the

Prince of Wales, himself a keen golfer, who had come to give the Cup away.

We saw him in the end presenting it to dear old J.H. Taylor, non-playing captain of the British team, almost beside himself with pride, and we saw Hagan with that impudent smile that captured so many male and female hearts saying, 'we had the Cup on our table on the Aquitania coming over and we had reserved a place for it going back'. Above all, we saw what was one of the most desperate finishes to any international match played to this day.

After two days of furious competition it all came down to one match: Sid Easterbrook against Densmore Shute. All square playing the last, Shute was perhaps 4½ feet from the hole in three, Easterbrook an inch or two inside him. Longhurst recalls the scene:

Shute, in the deathly silence that only comes from the presence of a vast multitude none of whom is making a sound, missed his putt. So now Easterbrook was left with his 4-footer, with a nasty left-hand borrow at that, and the complete golfer's nightmare – 'This for the entire match'. Even at the age of 24 I remember thinking, 'Better him than me'. Easterbrook holed it like a man, and the Cup was Britain's.

It would be another 22 years – with a world war in between – before Great Britain and Ireland would win the Cup again. By 1937 only Henry Cotton was a match for the Americans. He would win his singles, again at Southport and Ainsdale, as would a young Dai Rees, but our professionals were now only gathering the odd point at home as well as away. After the War in 1947, with a side full of ex-soldiers against a team, most of whom had been by-passed by the hostilities in Europe, Britain only won a single game. Sam King beat the

Masters Champion Herman Keiser, otherwise it was heavy defeats all the way from a US side full of post-war stars. Sam Snead, Ben Hogan, Byron Nelson, Jimmy Demaret, Lloyd Mangrum and Ed 'Porky' Oliver were now the backbone of a side whose constituent parts would dominate golf for a decade, indeed, until Arnold Palmer came along.

Britain and Ireland actually led after the foursomes in 1949 at Ganton, but won only a couple of points in the singles, Dai Rees again bucking the trend and building in his own mind the belief that Great Britain and Ireland could beat these So-and-Sos if only they played their own game and stopped being overawed. He would get his chance to prove his point as captain eight years later.

Hogan was back in the side of 1951, at Pinehurst, after a horrific car accident in 1949, from which few thought he would ever walk again, let alone play golf. But it wasn't sentiment that had him in the team. He had won the US Open at Merion the year after the accident and retained it in 1951. No surprise then that he won both his matches comfortably, as did most of the American team, the final score being a convincing 9½–2½.

The first time the home side really put up a commendable performance post-war was at Wentworth in 1953. Captained by Henry Cotton, they lost the foursomes 3–1, and by lunchtime on the second day it was clear they were once again heading for defeat by a significant margin. Then suddenly, for really no explicable reason, things started to go their way. Fred Daly who, along with Harry Bradshaw had won our only point in the foursomes with a 30-footer on the last green, went round the West Course in 66 in the morning, and finished off Ted Kroll by 9/7. Then Harry Weetman, 4 down and five to play against Sam Snead, won each of the last five holes for a most unexpected point.

Finally, the maths said that if Peter Alliss (1 down and one to play) could halve against Jimmy Turnesa, and if Bernard Hunt could beat Dale Douglas (on whom he was 1 up and one to play), the Cup would change hands. Again Henry Longhurst was there:

What ensued made a lasting mark on Alliss. One feels if he had quietly lost his match out in the country the rest of his golfing life might have been different. As it was, in the full ghastly light of publicity, not to be dimmed for many years, he took four from the edge of the green for a six, when even a five would have won the hole and halved the match. Alliss was only 22 at the time. Behind him, bringing up the rear, was Hunt, and as the evening shadows fell, he too took three putts and a six, when a five would have won him his match.

As has happened so often in these matches, and in its amateur counterpart the Walker Cup, on the rare occasion the chance to win comes long, we cannot take it. A bit like dropping slip catches when playing cricket against Australia.

Another one-sided match occurred in Palm Springs in 1955, notable only in that John Jacobs, later to be a renowned teacher, won both his matches. It was to be his only match. In 1953 he had won two of the four qualifying competition rounds around which that year's side was picked, yet did not make the team. In 1957, and having grown up at Lindrick where the match was played that year, and despite his fine deeds in Palm Springs, he didn't make that side either. To this day he feels he should have played three times, not just the once. Mind you, his 100 per cent record might have gone!

Then came 1957 and now it was Dai Rees's turn to be captain at home. Lindrick is almost an inland links, up there with the likes of Sunningdale as one of our great inland courses and certainly more familiar to us than to the Americans. After the foursomes it looked like more of the same though, with the US leading 3–1, only Dai Rees and Ken Bousfield winning their match. Dynamic action by Rees meant he left Harry Weetman and Max Faulkener out of the singles, much to the annoyance of the vociferous and vituperative Mrs Weetman! Nevertheless it was the right move.

Once again, let Longhurst take up the tale:

When the singles began, a whole succession of threes at the par 4 first appeared on the scoreboard. Yesterday, the same thing had happened but the threes were against the names of the Americans. This time they were against the names of the humble British. Cheer after cheer swept across the course as putts were holed and one could almost *feel* the uplift pervading the British team, far apart from each other as they might be. At the same time disintegration set in among the Americans and as a team they simply fell apart.

It was, beyond all doubt, a remarkable and well-merited victory for the British team, yet the taste of victory was not as sweet as it should, or might, have been. One member of the British team had the ill fortune to let fall an injudicious observation within hearing of a zealous journalist, who contrived to turn it overnight into a national 'incident'. The arrangements made for the American team were grossly inadequate and what they must have thought of us I do not care to think. When all was over, some did not even stay for the prize-giving and practically none turned up for the dinner.

Many things contrived to undermine the British team's effort to make a fight of it in 1959. They still crossed the Atlantic by boat in those days and even though it was on the *Queen Elizabeth*, it was a very rough trip and it was a ragged side that stumbled onto the dock in New York. There followed two or three days of receptions, travel and speech making before reaching Los Angeles. From there it was to be on a charter plane to Palm Springs – a trip of just a couple of hundred miles. Not long after take-off they ran into a thunderstorm, the tail-end of a hurricane that had been devastating Mexico. Their plane was tossed about for an hour, cabin luggage thrown everywhere, armrests broken and the stewardess knocked unconscious. They eventually made it back to Los Angeles and completed the journey by road. Those who were on that flight afterwards formed a club – the 'Long Drop Club' – and met annually for many years after to dine and thank providence for their deliverance.

It was no surprise that the British and Irish didn't put up much of a defence of the Cup so bravely won at Lindrick. The foursomes were quite close, but a number of heavy defeats in the singles meant that the result was never in doubt from fairly early on the second day. This was the last match played in the 36-hole format. For as long as team golf had been in existence, important matches had always been 36-hole affairs, whether it be Ryder Cup, Walker Cup, or the Oxford and Cambridge University Match. The trouble with these contests – especially when one side is much stronger than the other – is that games are frequently over by lunchtime. The situation is made worse by the 36-hole format, which favours the stronger player, giving him a chance to recover from a bad hole or two and impose his superiority.

From 1961, and by agreement of the two professional bodies, it was decided to have two 18-hole series of foursomes on the first day and the same for the singles on the second. About the same time, the Walker Cup also changed to the 18-hole format, but the Royal and Ancient and USGA, respectively responsible for the match either side of the Atlantic, agreed that it should be one foursomes and one singles each day and have played that way ever since.

In the Ryder Cup, where there had been only twelve points on offer, there were now 24, and while the individual matches were indeed closer, the overall result for the next few years was wider than ever. At Lytham in 1961 it was 14½–9½ and at Atlanta, two years later – fourballs having been introduced at the Americans' request, extending the match from two days to three and providing 32 points to play for – it was even wider. America won 23–9.

At Royal Birkdale in 1965 it was a bit closer, but not much, and with Arnold Palmer now fully into his stride and already with two Open Championships under his belt, America once more held all the aces. Two years later in Houston, Texas, saw the biggest US victory ever – 23½–8½ – and one wondered if these contests were ever going to be competitive again. These results were becoming downright embarrassing.

Then came Royal Birkdale in 1969 and finally we had a pied piper of our own to lead the charge. Tony Jacklin had for some time looked as though he could reach the very top of the game. By that year he'd won several tournaments back home and had taken his skills to America and won there too. He'd had the first televised hole-in-one in Britain, at Royal St Georges in the Dunlop Masters of 1967, and had a glamour as well as a golf game that really raised our hopes of international success after years in the golfing doldrums. Then, two months before the match, he had won The Open Championship just up the road at Royal Lytham and in doing so had lifted Britain's self-belief immeasurably.

Dai Rees had finally handed over the captain's banner to Eric Brown, a fiery and eccentric Scot, who had been part of that great team of 1957. His style was palpably aggressive and certainly the team went into the match full of ambitious intent. The first day's foursomes gave us a point lead, the morning being very good, the afternoon less so. The Americans came back to level the match at 8 points apiece after the fourballs and there was, by now, the feeling that we had enough good players to make a match of it on the final day. By lunchtime, victory was a real possibility. We had won that series 5 points to 3, and best of all, Tony Jacklin had beaten Jack Nicklaus 4/3.

These two would meet again in the afternoon, each in the anchor role for their respective sides. The pattern of that final set of singles was soon set. America took four of the first six games, Britain two; all games that went one way or the other early on, with none going to the 18th green. That left Brian Huggett playing Billy Casper all square coming up the last, with Jacklin and Nicklaus a hole behind.

As Huggett stood over his 4-foot putt to halve his game, a huge roar came from the 17th green. Naturally enough, Huggett thought that signalled another victory for Jacklin, and so leaving his putt for Britain to win the match. Brave as you like, he popped it in and promptly burst into tears on his captain's shoulder. Unfortunately, the roar was for a Jacklin eagle that had only been enough to bring his game level with one to play. So it was Jacklin versus Nicklaus down the 18th hole for the Ryder Cup.

No piece of golfing folklore has been replayed on screens around the world more often than those two on the green at Royal Birkdale in 1969. Both on the green in two, Jacklin first to putt, and gets it to some to 2 feet from the hole. Then Nicklaus, too bold and 5 feet past. Once again that deathly hush that only comes from an enormous crowd standing absolutely still and holding its breath. Nicklaus holed and with all the grace and charm that exemplified his career, and without a second thought, conceded Jacklin's putt with the immortal words: 'I don't for one minute think you would have missed it, but under the circumstances I wasn't going to give you the chance.' So came to an end a remarkable match, a tie, but still the Cup remained with the Americans, and the feeling lingered that perhaps this was a chance that had been missed and that might not come again for some time.

Indeed, Royal Birkdale 1969 did prove to be an exception to the rule of ongoing American domination. There was a bright start to the 1971 match at Old Warson, Missouri, Great Britain and Ireland leading by the odd point after the foursomes on day one. Sadly, a whitewash in the second morning fourballs and just a point and a half in the afternoon, and the Americans were back in familiar territory. The two series of singles were close, but the overall result was never in doubt.

At Muirfield in 1973, again Great Britain and Ireland led after the first day, only to stumble on the second afternoon. Tied going into the singles, they only managed to win one and halve four of sixteen matches played that day. As ever, when the Americans appear challenged, they never have any trouble in raising their game.

It was even worse in Arnold Palmer's backyard – Laurel Valley, Pennsylvania – two years later, where, after another whitewash in the foursomes on the first morning, Great Britain and Ireland barely scraped half the number of points the Americans amassed over the three days. All that bright hope surrounding Tony Jacklin's Open wins and the brave contest at Royal Birkdale in 1969 was fading fast.

It was about this time that Jack Nicklaus started floating his idea of broadening the catchment area for the Great Britain and Ireland team, if we really wanted it to be a serious contest. In 1977 at Royal Lytham, where once again the US cruised to a comfortable victory, he is on record as saying, 'The Americans are quite happy to treat this match as a goodwill gesture, a get together, a bit of fun. But here in Britain it's treated differently. The people here seem to want a serious, knock-em-down match. If that's what's wanted, there has to be stronger opposition. Something has to be done to make it more of a match for the Americans.'

While concurring with the thought that it would always be difficult for little old Great Britain and Ireland to find a dozen players to compete with the might of the United States, Nicklaus totally missed the point by saying it could just be a bit of fun: nothing is any fun if you are always on the losing side. And if it is always that one-sided, then it really is not worth playing anyway.

Nicklaus had originally aired his views a year or two previously to John Jacobs, who was at that time heavily involved in the splitting of professional golf into two separate bodies, one for the club pros and one for the tournament players The PGA remained the club profes-

sionals' body, while the tournament golfers set themselves up as the European Tour. At that time, Nicklaus
thought that the Ryder Cup ought to be the rest of the
world versus America, but that amorphous, nebulous
being – 'the Rest of the World' – never appealed, and
with the European Tour just coming into being, enlarg-
ing the match to be Europe versus America was the
obvious alternative step.

Nicklaus's acceptance that the addition of Europe
might make a difference was based on the emergence
of an extraordinary talent from the hills of Northern
Spain: Severiano Ballesteros. He had burst onto the
scene at Royal Birkdale in the summer of 1976, challenging all the way and only just failing to catch
America's Johnny Miller as he won The Open
Championship. None who saw it will ever forget the
deft little chip he played along a path between two
bunkers to the final green.

So, in 1979, it was Europe versus the United States,
and two Spaniards made the side – Seve, who had won
The Open at Royal Lytham that summer, and Antonio
Garrido. Neither, it must be said, made much impact
and Seve later revealed that, although he was aware of
the Ryder Cup, he knew little of its history and was little stirred by an event that involved much travel, some
forms of the game – foursomes – that were totally foreign to him, and, worst of all, there was no prize money.
Between them, Seve and Garrido managed only one
point from four goes in foursomes and fourballs, and
both lost their singles.

No surprise then that the outcome was little different
to when just Great Britain and Ireland by themselves
tried to take on the United States: 17–11 was the eventual margin. Worse, a couple of our team who should

have known better – Mark James and Ken Brown, both having played two years previously – took it on themselves to behave very poorly in the build-up to the match, in the process offending their captain, John Jacobs. It didn't escape the notice of the press. *The Daily Telegraph* coverage ran as follows:

The untoward events began before Europe flew from Heathrow, where Mark James turned up not wearing the approved uniform for the trip. John Jacobs, one of the chief begetters of the European Tour, had been chosen as captain and thought of sending James home.

During the flag raising ceremony he must have regretted his clemency, for the lounging attitude adopted by James and the young Scot, Ken Brown, amounted to rudeness both to hosts and comrades. They were also seen out shopping when Jacobs was holding team talks.

They continued to kick against the pricks for the duration of the match and afterwards both were fined: James £1,500 and Brown £1,000 – considerable sums in those days. Brown was also banned from playing in the match two years later. While there was no excuse for such behaviour, it was evidence of the low esteem in which some players held the way that their organisers put teams and their arrangements together. This was to provide the basis for changes demanded by Tony Jacklin some years later in return for his services as captain.

Both in 1979 and 1981, team selection was made by a committee of three: the Chairman of the Board of the Tour, Neil Coles, Jacobs as captain and the leader of the Order of Merit, who, in 1979, was Seve himself. Being new to the whole thing, Seve deferred to Jacobs, as did

Coles, and few would have argued with his choices of Peter Oosterhuis – by then playing full-time in America and quite successfully – and Des Smyth, who had recently won what would be the last *News of the World* Match Play Championship ever to be played.

1981, though, was very different. Seve Ballesteros was at odds with the European Tour over appearance money. That year, Lee Trevino and Tom Weiskopf both received $25,000 for playing in the Benson & Hedges at York, Weiskopf going on to win the tournament. European Tour players, however, could not accept appearance money and Seve virtually withdrew his services from the Tour for the whole of that year, even though Jacobs was in the throes of pushing through a special exemption clause for holders of major championships.

So Seve, having hardly played in Europe, had certainly not qualified as of right. Jacobs took it on himself to speak with each of the players who had made the team and canvassed their opinion as to whether they thought Seve should play. By now he had added the 1980 Masters to his Open victory at Lytham. With the exception of Bernard Gallacher – who believed everything that could be done, should be done to win the Ryder Cup – all felt Seve's participation would be wrong. He was omitted.

Another thorny problem was who should get the second captain's pick after Peter Oosterhuis, who was still near the top of his game but playing full time in America? It was between Mark James and Tony Jacklin, who were respectively 11th and 12th in the Order of Merit, with little to choose on that year's form. Jacklin, on his own admission, was well past his best, but in seven matches since 1967 had a pretty fair record.

James was a feisty match player well capable of holding his own. Selection was made at the end of August after the Benson & Hedges, where Jacklin had faltered somewhat on the run in. Bernard Langer was on the committee as that year's best player and both he and Coles felt James would now be the better bet in a close contest. So James it was.

It was a decision that would doubly offend Jacklin. Not only was he being passed over, but James was added to the team when the memory of his poor behaviour two years previously was still so fresh. Even so, in 1981 Europe was to go into the match without either of their iconic players from recent years, the only winners of major championships among their current players. It coincided with America sending over what may just have been their best side ever.

CHAPTER TWO

Jacklin's Revolution

1983
Tony Jacklin

The match at Walton Heath in 1981 might almost have sounded the death knell of the Ryder Cup. The addition of mainland Europe to our side hadn't made a blind bit of difference. Indeed, their presence seemed to have diminished the David versus Goliath element of past matches (where bright individual performances gave some pleasure against the awful one-sidedness of the whole thing) without adding much in return.

That year the match was supposed to have been played at The Belfry, but our new championship course, built in a bit of a hurry, had not matured sufficiently and for a month or two there was the unedifying sight of the event being hawked around, just to find somewhere to play. That those in charge of the Ryder Cup got a course as respected and renowned as Walton Heath – it had for many years been the home of the

Palm Beach Gardens

14–16 October

Europe (*Tony Jacklin*)	Matches		USA (*Jack Nicklaus*)
Foursomes: *Morning*			
B. Gallacher & A. Lyle	0	1	T. Watson & B. Crenshaw (5/4)
N. Faldo & B. Langer (4/2)	1	0	L. Wadkins & C. Stadler
J.M. Canizares & S. Torrance (4/3)	1	0	R. Floyd & B. Gilder
S. Ballesteros & P. Way	0	1	T. Kite & C. Peete (2/1)
Fourballs: *Afternoon*			
B. Waites & K. Brown (2/1)	1	0	G. Morgan & F. Zoeller
N. Faldo & B. Langer	0	1	T. Watson & J. Haas (2/1)
S. Ballesteros & P. Way (1 hole)	1	0	R. Floyd & C. Strange
S. Torrance & I. Woosnam (halved)	½	½	B. Crenshaw & C. Peete (halved)
Fourballs: *Morning*			
B. Waites & K. Brown	0	1	L. Wadkins & C. Stadler (1 hole)
N. Faldo & B. Langer (4/2)	1	0	B. Crenshaw & C. Peete
S. Ballesteros & P. Way (halved)	½	½	G. Morgan & J. Haas (halved)
S. Torrance & I. Woosnam	0	1	T. Watson & B. Gilder (5/4)
Foursomes: *Afternoon*			
N. Faldo & B. Langer (4/3)	1	0	T. Kite & R. Floyd
S. Torrance & J.M. Canizares	0	1	G. Morgan & L. Wadkins (7/5)
S. Ballesteros & P. Way (2/1)	1	0	T. Watson & B. Gilder
B. Waites & K. Brown	0	1	J. Haas & C. Strange (3/2)
Singles			
S. Ballesteros (halved)	½	½	F. Zoeller (halved)
N. Faldo (2/1)	1	0	J. Haas
B. Langer (2 holes)	1	0	G. Morgan
G.J. Brand	0	1	B. Gilder (2 holes)
A. Lyle	0	1	B. Crenshaw (3/1)
B. Waites	0	1	C. Peete (1 hole)
P. Way (2/1)	1	0	C. Strange
S. Torrance (halved)	½	½	T. Kite (halved)
I. Woosnam	0	1	C. Stadler (3/2)
J.M. Canizares (halved)	½	½	L. Wadkins (halved)
K. Brown (4/3)	1	0	R. Floyd
B. Gallacher	0	1	T. Watson (2/1)
Europe	13½	14½	**USA**

News of the World Match Play Championship and was one of those great Surrey and Berkshire heathland courses built in the early part of the 20th century – was fortunate indeed. It helped that Lord Aldington (formerly Sir Toby Lowe) was a member of the club and chairman of Sun Alliance, the first sponsor the Ryder Cup in Great Britain ever had.

Then the Americans arrived with possibly the finest side that ever left the United States. It was stuffed with multiple winners of major championships – Bruce Lietzke was the only member who would never win one – and there were all those tough nuts: Nicklaus, Trevino, Floyd, Irwin, Miller and Watson, all still very much at their peak. Larry Nelson was the last one to play his way into the side, by winning that year's US PGA Championship, and in his only previous match at the Greenbrier in 1979, had won 5 points out of 5. He would add another 4 from 4 at Walton Heath. What a 12th man!

Against them we seemed to have our weakest side for some years. Gone was the talismanic figure of Tony Jacklin (left out for the first time since 1967) and there was no Seve Ballesteros, who, after all, was the prime reason for Nicklaus suggesting Europe be included in the first place.

Jacklin's omission was also questionable. Captain John Jacobs had a couple of picks, one of whom was always going to be Peter Oosterhuis – by now playing full-time in America – and the final slot was between Jacklin and Mark James, who were numbers 11 and 12 in the list with less than £1,000 separating them. For James, with his misdemeanours from a couple of years earlier, to be preferred to Jacklin was a slight too far for the 1969 Open Champion. To no one's surprise he declined John Jacob's invitation to be one of his assistants. As far as Jacklin was concerned, he was finished with the Ryder Cup: 'By then I was totally disenchanted and particularly with the attitude of those in charge, not just of the Ryder Cup, but golf in Europe generally,' recalls Jacklin some 30 years on. 'For a dozen years or so, I had been playing mostly in the States, and was constantly aware of how much higher standards were over there. I am not talking about players' skills, but about the running of tournaments, the excellence of events week after week. The conditioning of the courses was far superior; they felt it important to get the greens as good as they could be. All the facilities were first class, the locker rooms, practice grounds, food in the clubhouse, all were absolutely as good as they could make them.

'Of course all this costs money and in those days the European Tour was nowhere near as well off as the US, but this wasn't just about money. No one was trying to raise standards and without raising those, then the standard of play wasn't going to improve either. And it wasn't just on the European Tour. I remember playing in the (British) Open Championship back then, and they didn't see the need to change the pin positions during the practice rounds. For three days you played to the same hole, which was always on the front of the green. For someone who played regularly in America, it all looked so unprofessional.

'The PGA [the club professional's body, rather than the European Tour, as it became after tournament players and club pros went their separate ways in 1973] headed up the Ryder Cup in those days, and it seemed to me they left so much to chance in putting a team together. It was travel as cheaply as possible – no wives or girlfriends then – find a company – any company – that might give you a few shirts, and off you go. If you wanted to take your own caddy, then you had to pay for him.

'I particularly remember one year, 1975 at Arnold Palmer's home club, Laurel Valley, we were all given Stylo's plastic shoes and one of my soles came completely off during my singles against Ray Floyd. Meanwhile, there they were, travelling by Concorde, looking a million dollars, wives to match and the best of everything laid on. In those days we really were second-class citizens and like lambs to the slaughter.

'Obviously, being me, I spoke my mind, but I was a lone voice and was always seen as something of a whinger. Once Peter Oosterhuis came along and later Nick Faldo, and started saying the same things, then they started listening, but throughout my playing days, despite what I had achieved, nothing changed. Then when Mark James was preferred to me in 1981, despite his dreadful behaviour at the Greenbrier, and then banning Seve, well, I thought I was done with the Ryder Cup. They just weren't serious about trying to win the match.

'Then in 1983 they came and asked me to be captain. I was in shock! It wasn't something I had anticipated; indeed I'd love to have known how they came to the decision. It was within a few months of the match and at the time I thought I must have been the choice of last resort. My first inclination, what with the way they went about putting a team into the field, and how little communication there was when I was left out, was to tell them to get lost. Overnight, though, I thought about how important the future of the European Tour was, how good it could be, and I didn't want to end my days in dispute with them and certainly not do anything that would drag them down.

'So I gave a lot of thought to all the things I felt should happen if our team was to go into the matches at least on a level footing. It wasn't that difficult. You looked at how they travelled, flying Concorde, and that would be how we should go. We should be properly dressed, plenty of shirts and trousers, good quality materials and suppliers. Of course you should have your own caddy and not cost you to have him there.

'The team room was something I instigated. For me, it was absolutely vital to have a room at the club or hotel where the team could get together and away from all the people who are inevitably around. Only there could a good team spirit be created and nurtured. In my day, playing under Eric Brown or Bernard Hunt, team get-togethers used to take place in some corner of the locker room; a quick huddle there, hope nobody was listening, and then we all went our separate ways, some to eat on their own, or with a chum, others to hit a few shots; the absolute opposite of creating cama- raderie and a sense of unity and purpose.

'A day or so after I had been asked to be the next cap- tain, I put all these issues on the table to Ken [Schofield, executive director of the Tour] and Colin [Snape, his opposite number at the PGA]. All the way through they kept saying "OK" and when I got to the end, nothing had been refused. Frankly, if they had said no to any of the big issues, then I would have just walked away, and with a clear conscience.'

With the match so close – less than six months away – the selection process for that year's team was already in place and had been announced. In earlier years the Ryder Cup committee, consisting of the chairman, the captain and the leader of the Order of Merit, had selected the final two players, the first ten coming off that year's money list. For 1983 the first twelve on that list would be the team: no committee or captain's picks.

This certainly didn't suit Jacklin: 'I obviously would have wanted some say in the make up of the team, but realised that late on it couldn't be changed. In any straight twelve players from the Order of Merit you are going to get some who just make it by gathering points from a lot of strokeplay tournaments. I have always believed there are those who enjoy the cut and thrust of matchplay more than others, but perhaps aren't consistent enough to play their way on. In 1983 I would have picked Manuel Pinero. He was one of the few who had a good match at Walton Heath, and has wonderful terrier-like qualities at matchplay.'

Seve Ballesteros was, of course, central to his cause, and even though he was back playing in Europe, animosity still lingered on. It was Lord Derby, President of the PGA and Chairman of the Ryder Cup committee, who realised how important a committed Seve Ballesteros was to Europe's chances and suggested that Tony Jacklin, and only Jacklin, should be the one to tackle Seve.

'I met with him at the Prince of Wales Hotel in Southport during The Open Championship at Royal Birkdale that year,' recalls Jacklin. 'He was still very much at odds with the European Tour and their attitude to appearance fees. He wasn't right on everything, but the Tour made very little effort to talk to him, to try and understand his point of view, and remember, he was their greatest asset, already had two majors under his belt, and Faldo and the rest hadn't come forward yet.

'I was passionate about the issue – him on the course and me doing all the other stuff – I thought we could make a real difference. I said to him, "Apart from anything else, your public relations in the UK is at rock bottom right now. If we can pull this off, turn this thing around, you will be seen by the British public as the greatest thing that ever happened." The long and the short of it was he saw the sense in what I said, recognised that however much he played in America, Europe would always be his base and this was a real opportunity to start moving forward rather than just looking back. From that chat in Southport he came aboard.'

One other issue mattered immensely to Jacklin – the format. Originally, both Ryder and Walker Cups had been played over two days (36-hole foursomes on day one and 36-hole singles on day two). In the early 1960s both matches were changed to four lots of 18-hole matches (two foursomes and two singles), in the hope that the shorter games might help the underdogs – us – have a better chance of winning a few more points. In return for this generosity in the Ryder Cup the US asked for their favourite form of the game, fourballs, to be included too. If they were going to go to all the trouble of putting a team together, and going all that way, then there should be a reasonable amount of golf at the end of it. Thus the event became a three-day affair from 1965 onwards.

Even within this framework the format changed from time to time – the number of matches per session, which day fourballs, which day foursomes. Sometimes there were two series of singles on the last day, sometimes just one. All the time there was an effort on both sides to try to make the contest more level, more competitive. In 1981 the format we now have – four foursomes and four fourballs on both the first two days and one series of singles on the last day, with all twelve players playing – was used for the first time.

'I thought this format, with just eight players out of the twelve playing at any one time the first couple of days was good for us', Jacklin remembers. 'All through my time as captain, they still had the strength in depth; any more games and our lack of depth would have been exposed. You could almost see that in the singles when everyone was playing and how hard it was for us to win. I suppose it was because they had such a strong team in 1981, they agreed. Later on they did ask for it to be changed to five games in each of the foursomes and fourballs, but I was convinced it was right to resist.'

So Jacklin had his agenda, but if you were to go out and purchase all he wanted, it would, even back then, have run into many tens of thousands of pounds. First-class air travel, a wardrobe full of designer golf wear – not to mention jackets and ties for the dress up evenings – then there were the wives and caddies, and it wasn't long before they had their uniforms for each and every function too. And remember, the Ryder Cup was still the sole responsibility of the PGA, the club professional's body, which was anything but flush, surviving as it did on the membership fees of club pros around the country, and whatever modest profit flowed from the Ryder Cup every four years.

It wasn't till the Ryder Cup became a sporting success, and shortly afterwards a huge commercial one as well, that the European Tour started to press the PGA for a share of the action, on the grounds that it was their players who were making the event so popular. Prior to that, at the time the tournament players parted company from the club pros in the early 1970s, the tournament players took the prestigious PGA Championship with them, leaving their erstwhile colleagues with the Ryder Cup, which at the time was of relatively little commercial value.

All Jacklin's requests were laid before Ken Schofield and Colin Snape, but it largely fell to Snape to make it happen. Jacklin was impressed by how well Snape succeeded: 'Colin started by going to BA and did a deal whereby if they laid on Concorde at a reasonable price, we would find 50 or so wealthy golf fanatics who would pay good money to fly Concorde, be with the team, included in photos, a sort of elite band of supporters, then that would take care of the cost of that; and it did. It became very much a joint effort; I was doing my bit on the team front, they did theirs making all things possible.

'Then they went to Austin Reed, who were happy to help out with the clothing; not free, but at a good price and in turn they got some good publicity out of it. That was the start. A few years later it was Burberry, and by now, with the match really taking off, they were most anxious for us to have their gear and then got Lord Patrick Litchfield to take the publicity pictures. And never forget, all this attention did wonders for the team's self-awareness and self-assurance; it was a case of I'd better pull my finger out if everyone's taking such an interest.

'To me, the amazing thing is that no one had ever bothered to try and make these sorts of things happen in the past; in the States it had been standard practice for years. Colin Snape, as I said, did most of it and was, I suppose, surprised and delighted he was able to achieve so much.

'I put a lot of thought into the team uniform, made

sure the colours I chose, and the combinations would look good on television. Vivien [Jacklin, Tony's first wife who so sadly died of a brain haemorrhage in 1988] helped me a lot with that, as she did in all areas where her knowledge was better than mine. I didn't discuss it with the players, this had to be put in place long before the final team was sorted; I just told them there were various outfits and which colours to wear on which day. Bearing in mind in the past they had been lucky to have more than a couple of shirts for the week, I suppose they were delighted. I certainly felt I left no stone unturned.

'With all this falling into place and with the match approaching, I took myself to West Palm Beach – the contest that year was at Palm Beach Gardens, home of the PGA of America and a massive complex of half a dozen courses and plenty of accommodation; not unlike The Belfry, but on a very grand scale. I looked at all the rooms where we would be staying, checked the suitability of the team room and how it would be serviced, changed a few things and flew home again. If you ask nicely, Americans are usually only too pleased to help and that was certainly the case here. Certainly no European captain had ever done this sort of reconnaissance before.

'Once we got close to the event I made it my business to go one-on-one with every player at some stage in the build up. I wanted them to understand that they could and must approach me if there was any issue on which they had a problem; that I was there for them to sort anything out that wasn't right. They had to know that was what I could do for them as captain.

'I can't say I learnt that much from previous captains I'd played under. I was impressed with Dai Rees's enthusiasm in my first match in 1967, and of course he had been the winning captain in 1957 when we won at Lindrick, so he went into the match believing the impossible might be achieved. Eric Brown at Birkdale in 1969 was all aggression: "don't help them look for their ball in the rough," that sort of thing, but mostly quite negative really.

'My one message to the team, once I had Seve on board for the first match in 1983, was that this thing was doable. Obviously as Faldo, Langer, Lyle Woosnam and Olazábal joined in and then picked up their majors, it was more than just doable. At the start it was just a continuation of my own attitude to golf in the 1960s and 1970s that any contest could be won and of course I had shown that to be true with my two Open wins; I did have some credibility.

'As for working out pairings and partnerships, in the beginning it was just close observation of people to see their reactions to one another, how comfortable they were in one another's company. That was very important to me, knowing they were going to be out there together under great pressure, some under the greatest pressure they were ever likely to face. If two people liked one another, got on well, then for me they had the makings of a good partnership, the whole could become greater than the sum of the parts, whether it be foursome or fourball.

'In 1983, I had no particular view as to how we might shape up against the Americans. I hadn't quite got the team I wanted because of the selection process, but with Seve on board once again, I felt we had the nucleus of a good team with some really good players coming through. Sandy Lyle was winning regularly, and often posting very low scores; Nick Faldo was clearly of a different class to much that had gone before in Europe, and Bernhard Langer could be among the very best if he could sort out his putting problems.

'Ian Woosnam, who had by then won a couple of tournaments and was a wonderful striker of the ball, looked to be a cut above the rest as well. The one player I might not have picked had I had any choice was Gordon J. Brand, who had got there through consistency rather than brilliance. He was twelfth in the standings when the team came together, and as I say, I was missing several players I might have preferred, Manuel Pinero and Howard Clark being two of them.'

What went on at Palm Beach Gardens was witnessed by very few. So one-sided had the matches become, US National television couldn't be persuaded to show it, so only the local channels were involved. We in Britain only got abbreviated coverage, but more on the final afternoon, when there was a chance we might win: even so, it was only the last two or three holes. It was mid-October, but stifling hot, and with those who winter in Florida having not yet arrived, there were few spectators.

Even against the might of America's 1981 side, Europe had led after the first day, and the same was true this time – a point ahead at 4½–3½. Sam Torrance – a bit of a late developer at 30 years old – hadn't had a happy time on his first outing at Walton Heath, but got an immediate point with José Maria Canizares. Then, in what was Ian Woosnam's first ever game in the Ryder Cup, Torrance took the honour in the fourballs and promptly hit his first drive out of bounds. A tough baptism, but Woosnam was up to it and a few hours later they put half a point on the board.

In hindsight, the pairing of Nick Faldo and Bernhard

Langer would appear to be a banker, but both were still a long way short of reaching their potential. Faldo had had a dream introduction to the Ryder Cup at Royal Lytham in 1977, partnering Peter Oosterhuis to wins in both foursomes and fourballs and then beating Tom Watson in the singles. The word precocious was everywhere bandied about. That morning they comfortably saw off Lanny Wadkins and Craig Stadler, and would win twice more before the singles.

The real success for Jacklin's embryonic captaincy was the pairing of Ballesteros and Paul Way: 'Paul was only 21 at the time, and reminded me a lot of myself at that age; bold, brash and great self-belief. Most important he was inspired by playing with Seve. Yes, he was in awe of him, but not overawed by him. They were the classic master and pupil combination.' They lost their first foursome, but soon gelled to produce 2½ points from their next three games.

At one point another Spaniard, Angel Gallardo, called Jacklin over saying Seve had a problem: 'It was lunchtime on the second day, and Seve was in the locker room changing for the afternoon. And he says, "Tony, this boy; I am having to hold his hand. I have to tell him everything, what shot to play, what club to hit. I feel like his father."

'"Seve," I replied, "in his mind, to him, out here, you are his father. You are the great Seve Ballesteros, you've won two majors. You know everything. Do you have a problem with that?"

'"Of course," said Seve, chest swelling, "it is no problem,"' and off he went to win another point.

'I like to think that was the point Seve finally came to understand and appreciate what the Ryder Cup was all about; the comradeship, the responsibility, the passion and the fun of taking on and beating the Americans. So very much more than just playing for yourself in another tournament.'

The US fought back on day two and eventually squared the contest going into the singles. But in many ways that was the crucial day for Jacklin's captaincy: the day when, in the past, so many promising starts had foundered, but not this time. They were still there with all to play for and some very good players with whom to do it.

Historically, at least in the Americans' minds, you put your top players out at the end, in the singles, in order to take care of business should it get tight. We had more or less gone along with that. Think of Jacklin and Nicklaus going out last twice on the last day at Birkdale in 1969: 'I had given much thought to my singles line up, knowing what they would probably do. I wanted Seve out top, leading the way, the captain on the field. That was how I always saw him and that was where he should be. Then I put Faldo and Langer out next, and so on. When we opened the envelopes on the evening before, Jack nearly fell off his chair. "You can't do that!" he said, "Why not?" I replied, "what's the point of having Seve at the bottom, if the match is already over? I want his point to count, and count early."'

For a time, on the day, this ploy worked well. Seve was soon a couple up on Fuzzy Zoeller, and Faldo and Langer were doing much the same. Elsewhere there was not much in it, though Ken Brown quickly eased away from Ray Floyd, and Bernard Gallacher seemed to have the edge over Tom Watson – those matches being the bottom two.

One comment to note that afternoon came from the much-loved American commentator, Dave Marr. Craig

Stadler was proving too good for Ian Woosnam, but being the size he is, the Walrus was soon sweating profusely, so much so that his elegant pink shirt was turning a dark red: 'That's what comes of being dressed by the dreaded sisters, Polly and Esther,' observed the droll Marr in his deep southern accent.

In these early days of Jacklin's stewardship – and long before anyone could guess just how glorious it would become – Seve was very much the lightening conductor for the team, its talisman. Suddenly his star that day began to wane. Three up and seven to play, he evaporated to the point where he was 1 down playing the last. Then he drove in a bunker at 18, a par-5. Zoeller couldn't get up in two, but Seve just managed it. A 3-wood from some 240 yards found the green and his match was halved. He is forever remembered for that heroic shot, somehow symbolic of Europe's new-found fighting spirit, but it was a match he really should have won.

Torrance, too, might have won, but Kite finished well to share the spoils in that one. So it was down to the last two games, and the match could still be won if Gallacher and Canizares could somehow muster a point and a half between them. Gallacher had lost his early advantage and was now 1 down and two to play against Watson. Canizares was all square playing the last against Lanny Wadkins.

In trouble all the way up the last, Wadkins hit his approach dead from 60 yards and escaped with a half, while Gallacher made a mess of the 17th and America were through on home soil by the narrowest of margins: 14½–13½. So relieved was Nicklaus not to have become the first American captain to lose at home, he knelt down and kissed the spot from which Wadkins had hit that last shot. However, it was only shame delayed. He would collect that unenviable distinction a mere four years later.

'We went very close that day,' Jacklin reflects, 'and frankly were unlucky to lose. Deep down we all felt it was a match we'd let get away. Look at the photographs taken afterwards, and there we all are with glum faces. Perhaps in the end we hadn't really believed enough it was possible. But the great thing was we had shown ourselves that this match really was winnable with the players we had; it was definitely a springboard for the next match at The Belfry. As Seve said at the end, "This wasn't a loss, this was a win, just to have got so close".'

The Belfry

13–15 September

Europe (*Tony Jacklin*)	Matches		USA (*Lee Trevino*)
Foursomes: *Morning*			
S. Ballesteros & M. Pinero (2/1)	1	0	C. Strange & M. O'Meara
B. Langer & N. Faldo	0	1	C. Peete & T. Kite (3/2)
A. Lyle & K. Brown	0	1	L. Wadkins & R. Floyd (4/3)
H. Clark & S. Torrance	0	1	C. Stadler & H. Sutton (3/2)
Fourballs: *Afternoon*			
P. Way & I. Woosnam (1 hole)	1	0	F. Zoeller & H. Green
S. Ballesteros & M. Pinero (2/1)	1	0	A. North & P. Jacobsen
B. Langer & J.M. Canizares (halved)	½	½	C. Stadler & H. Sutton (halved)
S. Torrance & H. Clark	0	1	R. Floyd & L. Wadkins (1 hole)
Fourballs: *Morning*			
S. Torrance & H. Clark (2/1)	1	0	T. Kite & A. North
P. Way & I. Woosnam (4/3)	1	0	H. Green & F. Zoeller
S. Ballesteros & M. Pinero	0	1	M. O'Meara & L. Wadkins (3/2)
B. Langer & A. Lyle (halved)	½	½	C. Stadler & C. Strange (halved)
Foursomes: *Afternoon*			
J.M. Canizares & J. Rivero (7/5)	1	0	T. Kite & C. Peete
S. Ballesteros & M. Pinero (5/4)	1	0	C. Stadler & H. Sutton
P. Way & I. Woosnam	0	1	C. Strange & P. Jacobsen (4/2)
B. Langer & K. Brown (3/2)	1	0	R. Floyd & L. Wadkins
Singles			
M. Pinero (3/1)	1	0	L. Wadkins
I. Woosnam	0	1	C. Stadler (2/1)
P. Way (2 holes)	1	0	R. Floyd
S. Ballesteros (halved)	½	½	T. Kite (halved)
A. Lyle (3/2)	1	0	P. Jacobsen
B. Langer (5/4)	1	0	H. Sutton
S. Torrance (1 hole)	1	0	A. North
H. Clark (1 hole)	1	0	M. O'Meara
N. Faldo	0	1	H. Green (3/1)
J. Rivero	0	1	C. Peete (1 hole)
J.M. Cañizares (2 holes)	1	0	F. Zoeller
K. Brown	0	1	C. Strange (4/2)
Europe	**16½**	**11½**	**USA**

CHAPTER THREE

Victory Anticipated

1985
Tony Jacklin

By 1985 The Belfry was still something of an ugly duckling. It had matured sufficiently to be suitable to hold the match, but was still a long way from being the polished, pristine article it is today. That the Ryder Cup was to be played there on the next three occasions the match came to Britain deeply offended traditionalists. With all our great links courses, the inland beauties to the south-west of London and the various other historic venues dotted around the country, surely, they said, the Ryder Cup was worthy of more than repeated visits to this converted potato patch.

It was, however, perfect for Tony Jacklin's purposes. After the fine job he had done in Florida, he was soon reappointed as captain and asked to have a second go at home: 'I worked with Brian Cash, chief executive of The Belfry, for the best part of eight months setting up an atmosphere which guaranteed we had our own rooms to eat together, relax together and above all, complete privacy; almost a family atmosphere you might say.

'Brian was a great help. He believed in excellence as much as I did. He understood that the better we did, the better it would reflect on his hotel. He provided everything I asked for and more. We got the rooms we asked for and he provided every sort of food and drinks the players wanted. Of course there was no reason for the players not to gravitate to the team room and it was there that the team came together.

'Right from the start I felt it important that the players' wives should be part of what we were doing. I am certain their presence at The Belfry was a big factor in creating the atmosphere of togetherness I believed so essential. I could never have achieved what I did without the help and support of my wife Vivien, and after she so sadly died, with Astrid. One of the reasons I accepted the captain's job a fourth time in 1989 was so Astrid could experience this extraordinary event and see why it meant so much to me.'

The Belfry was soon to prove itself in other ways. After the close encounter in 1983, interest and anticipation were enormous. The sheer rarity of these matches – there are eight major championships between each one – whets the appetite as much as the closeness of the contests. Suddenly the Ryder Cup was the must-have ticket, and The Belfry was one of those rare inland courses that had the space to cope. Also, being at the heart of Britain's motorway system, everyone could get there.

Peter Alliss and Dave Thomas had designed the course specifically for tournament play, and to be

American in style, so that – should any of our players be good enough to go and play over there – they would at least have had some experience of the conditions they were likely to meet. Even though it was deemed unready for the Ryder Cup in 1981, a tournament had been held there every year from 1979 – first the English Open and then the Lawrence Batley.

Although Jacklin would have had no say in the choice of venue, a regular tournament at the course where the match was going to be played would have been high on his list of priorities. Local knowledge was an advantage not lightly cast aside. And as Peter Oosterhuis, who had been ten years in the States plying his trade, and who had played The Belfry the summer before the match, said: 'Don't worry about the American look of the course, it is still hard and bouncy and it will drive them mad.'

What Jacklin could do was have the course set up to suit the European players as much as possible, something that had never been considered before. 'There wasn't a great deal to do, but I made sure there would be none of that fluffy long grass close to greens that was the staple diet for Americans; I had all the areas round the greens shaved so you could chip, something they don't get to do very often. Then I made sure the speed of the greens were right for our side, so quite a bit slower than they were used to.'

For Jacklin, this Ryder Cup match was almost a continuation of what he had started in Florida; as though there was no time lapse between the end of one and the start of the next: 'The only thing we had done wrong there was not win the match. We had played well, lost by the narrowest of margins, and, most important of all, proved to ourselves this was a contest we were good enough to win.

'Rather than a two-year gap, it was like we had shot 66 in the first round of a major and were just setting out for the second. I was struck by this feeling of continuity during our last practice rounds at The Belfry. I suppose I had been worrying away at it for the best part of eighteen months, ever since I was reappointed captain. From that moment I was forever watching tournament results, checking the form of the obvious candidates, as the team gradually emerged.'

By this time Jacklin had put in place the one ingredient missing in 1983. He had sole and final say over the composition of the team. Back then he had been appointed too late to influence the selection procedure. Now he had three picks to add to the nine who qualified via the Order of Merit. Previously, there had been no more than a couple of wildcard choices for captain and committee, but more of our players were now playing in the US and nothing they did over there counted towards the European team. Nick Faldo was an obvious case in point. Jacklin also had strong views on who might be the better competitor in the cut-and-thrust cauldron of the Ryder Cup, as opposed to the more genteel atmosphere of a four-round medal.

Christy O'Connor Jnr was the unlucky one in 1985, as Jacklin reached for Faldo, the experienced Ken Brown and José Rivero. In selecting Rivero – at that time twelfth in the list of eligible players – he would have been influenced by Seve Ballesteros. Ballesteros was a fan of his fellow Spaniard and intimated to Jacklin that together they could be a winning combination in foursomes and fourballs. With Manuel Pinero and José Maria Canizares also in the side, this gave the captain a couple of Spanish pairs to put into the field – their intense sense of nation would have meant they were playing as much for Spain as for Europe: 'It had been my intention to pair Seve with Rivero, but after thirteen holes in the practice round I could see it was not working. I do not know if playing with Seve undermined Rivero's confidence a bit; if he was in awe of him, or what. So, I pulled Pinero out of his partnership with Canizares and put him in with Seve for the last five holes of practice.'

While confidence and self-belief had been boosted by the match in Palm Beach, so had public expectation. Being favourites was not something that passed anyone's lips, not after all those years of heavy hammerings and dashed hopes, but with the team stronger than before and with home advantage, this surely was the best chance we'd ever had.

Surprisingly, at the opening ceremony, Jacklin's opposite number, Lee Trevino, was, for all his bombast as a player, strangely muted. Maybe he felt his usual wisecracking ways would not be suitable on such an occasion, and when he introduced his players it was by name only, no flamboyance. Jacklin, on the other hand, was not to be restrained: 'Sandy Lyle ... Open Champion, Bernhard Langer ... US Masters Champion ... and Seve Ballesteros ... the greatest golfer in the World.' Round one to Jacklin.

Trevino would appear to have brought little to the role of captain other than as organiser and enabler. Throughout the practice days he hid behind dark glasses and gave little away at press conferences. None of his usual ebullience was on show. If any American was to bring passion to the job of captain, you would expect it of Trevino, but not on this occasion. For more than half a century Americans had been able to win this thing without getting their hands dirty or breaking sweat. The big European surge had not yet started and Trevino saw no need for change.

Such was the interest in the Ryder Cup, now that we seemed to have a real chance, even the BBC cleared its decks as far as it was able. These were the early days of breakfast television and Frank Bough introduced the Friday show in front of The Belfry Hotel, with special guests Peter Alliss and Bruce Forsyth. It was a cold, grey cold mid-September. Dawn had scarcely broken.

Perhaps surprisingly, Jacklin had broken up his most successful partnership from the 1983 match, Seve Ballesteros and Paul Way. Way had started the year well, winning the PGA Championship and qualifying early for the team. Then, midsummer, he contracted tonsillitis, couldn't play for several weeks and was scarcely fit by the time the match started, so he was very much an unknown quantity.

More important, Seve had indicated he would like to play with a fellow Spaniard, and while it wasn't to be his original choice, José Rivero, Manuel Pinero was a more-than-adequate substitute. Together they led Europe off in the first series of foursomes, and a fine job they did: 2/1 victors over Curtis Strange and Mark O'Meara. Elsewhere though, it was a horror story. No match went past the 17th green and America won them all.

Jacklin had put Bernhard Langer and Nick Faldo together again – after all, they had won 3 points out of 4 two years previously. This time though, Faldo was in the midst of his well documented swing changes, and neither his golf nor his mood was conducive to good team golf. Three over par through eleven holes meant 4 down and eventual defeat by 3/2.

Jacklin – ever the good man-manager – asked Faldo if he wanted another go or should he bring Canizares in to partner Langer? Faldo excused himself, didn't play again till the singles and lost that too, to one of America's lesser lights, Hubert Green. On paper, Faldo would have been one of Jacklin's trump cards, but in 1985 his golf wasn't good enough to deliver a single trick.

Europe 1, the United States 3, had not been in the script, but Jacklin didn't panic: 'I didn't come the heavy stuff. There were no pep talks, no recriminations. We just had a frank discussion about the way every player was feeling inside. Quite a few players were not fond of foursomes and were looking forward to hitting their own ball in the afternoon. Despite the scoreline, I felt we went out optimistic and determined.'

This time Ian Woosnam and Paul Way went out first – a couple of birdie machines, who might have been perceived as a little erratic for the precise art of foursomes. But they did exactly what was required of them, going round in a better ball score of 64 – even so, it was only just good enough to beat Fuzzy Zoeller and Hubert Green on the last green. They had been 3 up after ten, thus fulfilling an important task for those who go first – that is, to get positive figures on the board early, in order to encourage the rest. However, they were hauled back to all square and two to play, only for Way to win the 18th with a birdie 3. Way's health was no longer an issue.

Seve and Pinero duly delivered another point, and Langer and Canizares had a fine match against Craig Stadler and Hal Sutton – never more than a hole in it, halves at the last five holes and the match finishing all square. One point behind after the first day was somehow a great improvement on two down at lunch. Only Howard Clark and Sam Torrance lost both matches that first day, but a fourball loss on the last green to Ray Floyd and Lanny Wadkins, despite going round in 67, was no disgrace. Jacklin persevered with them the following morning and would be repaid for his trust with a victory.

Europe was now into its stride on what was to prove a momentous Saturday. Almost for the only time in the history of these matches, the order of play was reversed for the second day. On Friday the first series had been foursomes, with fourballs in the afternoon. Now, on Saturday, it was to be fourballs first and foursomes after lunch. Clark and Torrance were given the spearhead role and did as Way and Woosnam had done the previous afternoon – got an early lead and kept it. Way and Woosnam also played well again and soon had a second point on the board. Europe was now ahead for the first time in the match.

For once there was no sparkle from Seve and Pinero: level par to the turn is not good enough in fourball better ball, and they were 4 down to Mark O'Meara and Lanny Wadkins. A point back for America and the match level again, with one game left out. Bernhard Langer and Sandy Lyle had won the 1st hole but soon trailed Craig Stadler and Curtis Strange, and it looked as though Europe's bright start to the day would be wiped out. Eventually, the Americans were 2 up and two to play.

The 17th at The Belfry is a 575-yard dog-leg par-5, reachable in two by the very longest hitters but only if they manage to cut the corner and hold the fairway. Neither of the Americans could get there in two, but a pitch stone-dead from Stadler looked to have finished the match. Lyle, though, had found the green in two and holed from some 20 feet for an eagle – game still alive.

At the 18th, both Langer and Lyle had birdie chances, but neither holed and it was left to Stadler to finish things off with a putt for the match from no more than 18 inches. At any other time such a short one would almost certainly be conceded, but as it was for the match ... And Stadler missed! For the very first time in the history of these contests, and certainly within living memory, an American had cracked. Ask anyone who had watched these matches down the years when it was that the tide finally turned, and most would cite that missed putt by Stadler on the second morning in 1985. It certainly broke the Americans that day and that week. Jacklin led off the afternoon foursomes with his two Spanish pairings and within a couple of hours they had thrashed their opponents: Canizares and Rivero winning by 7/5 against Tom Kite and Calvin Peete, Ballesteros and Pinero by 5/4 against Stadler and Sutton.

Way and Woosnam deserved their place in the foursomes, having won two fourball matches, but found the straightjacket of this more demanding format too restraining. They bogied four holes round the turn and lost comfortably to Peter Jacobsen and Curtis Strange. However, Europe finished on a high when Langer and Ken Brown beat the daunting combination of Floyd and Wadkins by 3/2. The gloom of the first morning had been replaced by the euphoria of a 2-point lead with the singles to come.

'I have always felt the right philosophy for the singles is to put most of your best players out early to get their result and hopefully their win on the board quickly,' recalls Jacklin some 25 years later. 'Then keep some strength and experience to the end, should things get tight. That's what I did in 1983, but at The Belfry I put most of the cream in the middle. I was sure Trevino would put his best players out first to try and get back into the match as soon as possible. That is exactly how it worked out.'

Jacklin didn't exactly neglect the top. While Manuel Pinero would not have been in the top echelon of his side, Jacklin rated his match-playing qualities highly: 'He's like a terrier, always at your heels, a great match player. He's like Gary Player, a little man, but a tremendous fighter. And you know Nicklaus never beat Player in a match. He was thrilled when I asked him to go out first, and when he saw he was playing Wadkins [still the American with the best Ryder Cup record of all], he nearly jumped a foot in the air.'

The singles in the Ryder Cup usually start at 11 am. On that September morn, with Europe leading and with a real chance of winning for the first time in nearly 30 years, all 25,000 ticket-holders were in before the first shot was struck. By the time Pinero and Wadkins walked onto the 1st tee, the entire 1st hole was ringed five or six deep. It has a slightly raised tee, and it would have looked to those two players as though they were driving into a small green pond surrounded by a terrace of humanity.

Wadkins is all cocky self-assurance, with a swagger and a quick flashy swing. He is known to have greeted earlier and lesser opponents in Ryder Cup matches with, 'Hello, lunch!' What he said to Pinero that day is not recorded. What is known is that, at the end of a scrappy front nine, with both players approximately a couple over par, the match was square. Then Pinero chipped in at 10 to go 1 up and birdied 11 to make it 2. That effectively was that. Wadkins wilted and the match ended with Pinero winning the 17th for victory by 3/1.

Behind them, Woosnam lost to Stadler, but Paul Way then beat Ray Floyd on the 18th and Trevino's strategy of getting points on the board early was in tatters. The Americans might have got back into things when Tom Kite was 3 up on Ballesteros with just six to play, but Seve rallied to gain a half, and after that it was a question of who would hole the putt to win the Ryder Cup.

It could have been Howard Clark, who had a putt on the 17th to beat O'Meara 2/1, but that slipped by. All eyes then turned to Sam Torrance, who was playing the last against Andy North. Like Seve, Torrance had been behind all the way, at one point 3 down and eight to play, but he, too, had rallied, and had won the 17th to square the match. When Torrance found the fairway at 18, North faltered and pulled his drive into the pond. That surely was that, but Sam gave us the grandstand finish. With tears already running down his face he found the green in two and then holed from 20 feet – a putt that must have been shown more often than any in the history of the game.

Jacklin's team had achieved what he had always felt was eminently possible. He had imbued the Europeans with tremendous self-belief and they had responded brilliantly to his inspired captaincy. It was a magic moment in golf made all the more dramatic when Concorde, that triumph of European aeronautical achievement flew in low over The Belfry in a unique victory salute.

So the dragon had been slain, and Tony Jacklin had given us a blueprint of how it could be done again and again. But he still had one more mountain to climb: to be the first man to captain a European side to victory in America. He was to have his chance two years later.

1987 – Muirfield Village

25–27 September

Europe (*Tony Jacklin*)	Matches		USA (*Jack Nicklaus*)
Foursomes: *Morning*			
S. Torrance & H. Clark	0	1	C. Strange & T. Kite (4/2)
K. Brown & B. Langer	0	1	H. Sutton & D. Pohl (2/1)
N. Faldo & I. Woosnam (2 holes)	1	0	L. Wadkins & L. Mize
S. Ballesteros & J.M. Olazábal (1 hole)	1	0	L. Nelson & P. Stewart
Fourballs: *Afternoon*			
G. Brand Jnr & J. Rivero (3/2)	1	0	B. Crenshaw & S. Simpson
A. Lyle & B. Langer (1 hole)	1	0	A. Bean & M. Calcavecchia
N. Faldo & I. Woosnam (2/1)	1	0	H. Sutton & D. Pohl
S. Ballesteros & J.M. Olazábal (2/1)	1	0	C. Strange & T. Kite
Foursomes: *Morning*			
J. Rivero & G. Brand Jnr	0	1	C. Strange & T. Kite (3/1)
N. Faldo & I. Woosnam (halved)	½	½	H. Sutton & L. Mize (halved)
A. Lyle & B. Langer (2/1)	1	0	L. Wadkins & L. Nelson
S. Ballesteros & J.M. Olazábal (1 hole)	1	0	B. Crenshaw & P. Stewart
Fourballs: *Afternoon*			
N. Faldo & I. Woosnam (5/4)	1	0	C. Strange & T. Kite
E. Darcy & G. Brand Jnr	0	1	A. Bean & P. Stewart (3/2)
S. Ballesteros & J.M. Olazábal	0	1	H. Sutton & L. Mize (2/1)
A. Lyle & B. Langer (1 hole)	1	0	L. Wadkins & L. Nelson
Singles			
I. Woosnam	0	1	A. Bean (1 hole)
H. Clark (1 hole)	1	0	D. Pohl
S. Torrance (halved)	½	½	L. Mize (halved)
N. Faldo	0	1	M. Calcavecchia (1 hole)
J.M. Olazábal	0	1	P. Stewart (2 holes)
E. Darcy (1 hole)	1	0	B. Crenshaw
J. Rivero	0	1	S. Simpson (2/1)
B. Langer (halved)	½	½	L. Nelson (halved)
A. Lyle	0	1	T. Kite (3/2)
S. Ballesteros (2/1)	1	0	C. Strange
G. Brand Jnr (halved)	½	½	H. Sutton (halved)
K. Brown	0	1	L. Wadkins (3/2)
Europe	**15**	**13**	**USA**

CHAPTER FOUR

Irresistible in America

1987 and 1989
Tony Jacklin

By 1987 the formula for producing European teams in mint condition for the match, and containing the twelve best players available, was well established. Where, four years earlier, Tony Jacklin and officials from the PGA and European Tour had to beat down doors to get support, now sponsors were falling over themselves to get a piece of this new success story. Johnnie Walker was the team sponsor, Austin Reed were making much sweeter noises about producing the requisite clothing, and the big entertainment agency of the day, Keith Prowse, had taken over the bothersome job of selling off spare seats on Concorde at £5,000 a time, enabling players and officials to travel free. Amazing what a win can do!

How quickly things change. After flying direct to Columbus, Ohio, Jacklin and his team descended the steps in their new £600-cashmere jackets to be greeted by Jack Nicklaus. On shaking hands Nicklaus fingered the material of Jacklin's jacket, raised his eyebrows but said nothing. Two days later the American team had new jackets too, and you can guess the cloth.

And it wasn't only in clothing that the Americans were now having to play catch up. Not long after The Belfry result was in, Nicklaus – already chosen to be captain at his own course, Muirfield Village – began seeking changes to the American team's selection process. He realised the importance of having the best players in the team, especially proven matchplay winners. He got the selection period extended to two years, believing this would give the likes of Ray Floyd, Tom Watson and Lanny Wadkins the best chance of making the team. But that didn't work, as only Wadkins played his way in.

Later, once the match got underway and America fell behind again, Nicklaus began questioning the sense of the US Open Champion and the US PGA qualifying as of right. Was one week's good play, however big the event, the right way to allocate two of the places, when everyone else was having to spend two years doing it? The fact that the two major winners in his team that year were Scott Simpson and Larry Nelson might have had something to do with it. Simpson did little else in his career except win one US Open and finish runner-up in another, and Nelson was nowhere near the player he had been six years earlier. Nicklaus was beginning to discover that losing isn't nearly so much fun as winning.

Understandably Nicklaus has been captain of more American teams than anyone else. He played through those great years when just turning up meant victory for the US. His style of captaincy reflected those comfy,

Rolls Royce years. He has always seen the job of captain as largely ambassadorial, believing that just by qualifying for the side you have proven yourself to be competent and competitive enough to know how to prepare.

Not for Nicklaus the stirring of the pot of glue so essential for creating a single competitive unit out of twelve disparate parts. He hasn't always been a winning captain but has never changed his views on how the job should be done. When asked by Paul Azinger, the 2008 Ryder Cup captain, for any advice, he told him he should get rid of all this nonsense of vice-captains and sidekicks, and just make sure that the team lacked for nothing. Azinger did not follow Jack's advice in one respect. He chose three vice-captains, two of whom have been pretty successful in the job themselves, Dave Stockton and Raymond Floyd.

In 1986, a year before the Muirfield Village match, and under the guise of needing changes to bring American television to the party – something that would have mattered greatly to him as the owner and promoter of this fine facility – Nicklaus suggested altering the format, extending the event to four days to include two sets of singles. In those days, any extension of time or content would have exposed Europe's acknowledged lack of depth. Wisely, as holders of the trophy, Jacklin and the PGA rejected the suggestion and the format has remained unchanged to this day – and American television now shows every shot on every day!

Meanwhile, Jacklin was more than happy with the team that emerged to defend the trophy in Nicklaus' back yard. He still had nine of those who had won so well at The Belfry, and while he would have loved to have had Manuel Pinero, José Maria Canizares and Paul

Way had they been playing well enough to make the team, he was thrilled with the arrival of José Maria Olazábal. Olazábal and Sandy Lyle both had to be selected by Jackson as so much of their time was spent on the US Tour and his third choice, Ken Brown, was also dividing his time between the US and Europe. Gordon Brand Jnr (no relation to the Gordon J. Brand, who played in 1983) was a feisty addition and only Eamonn Darcy would have given mild cause for concern, as he had played in only a couple of Ryder Cups some years before and was yet to win a point. Against that, Nick Faldo was back to his best, and had won The Open Championship earlier in the year.

So it was a confident and expectant Europe that stepped onto the 1st tee for the first series of foursomes that fine September morning in 1987. Within a couple of hours though, Europe was down in all four matches. Once again it was foursomes – a form of golf invented by the British and thought to be our speciality – that was the cause of the problem.

In the top game, Sam Torrance and Howard Clark lost three of the first five holes and went on to lose by 4/2. It was much the same for Bernhard Langer and Ken Brown who, despite winning the 1st hole, lost four of the next ten and were beaten 2/1. That first morning Jacklin had put his real power out in the bottom two games, Faldo and Woosnam, playing together for the first time, as were José Maria Olazábal and Seve Ballesteros. Foursomes is a hard discipline to settle into, but both pairs got the hang of it before holes ran out and both turned their respective games around. It was a relieved Jacklin that sat down to lunch that day, with a share of points from the first series.

For the afternoon fourballs, Torrance and Clark were

rested and replaced by Brand Jnr and José Rivero. Ken Brown made way for Sandy Lyle, who was still regarded as a bit erratic for foursomes, but had just what it takes for fourballs – lots of birdies and eagles. The pairing of Brand Jnr and Rivero shows that, despite Jacklin's well publicised determination to play all his big name players in every series – as he did in each of his four years as captain – he was also mindful of giving everyone a game before the singles: 'I just didn't think it was fair to ask anyone to go out there cold on that last day, in front of all those people and expect them to perform. Provided they played once, they knew that I was going to rely on maybe just 50 per cent of the team to deliver 60/70 per cent of the points, bearing in mind this handful of major champions I had at my disposal.'

True to his word, once he had the selection of teams where he wanted it, every one of his players always got at least one game over the first two days. The only player to miss out during his time was Gordon J. Brand in 1983 and Jacklin had the honesty to say in the plane going over that not everyone would necessarily get to play before the singles. Also, the atmosphere at Palm Beach Gardens was nothing compared with what came two years later – and that has remained ever since.

That first afternoon, Brand Jnr and Rivero took full advantage of their opportunity, beating Ben Crenshaw – at that time possibly the best putter in the game – and the aforementioned Scott Simpson. They were heading for a better ball score of 66 or 67 when they won on the 16th green.

The three other pairings that Friday afternoon then established themselves as the foundation on which Jacklin would push on to victory. Lyle joined Langer and they were somewhat lucky to win, their opponents,

Mark Calcavecchia and Andy Bean, dropping shots at both 17 and 18 – and remember this is fourballs – and going from 1 up and two to play to a one-hole loss. In years gone by that sort of collapse was almost the private preserve of British teams: now, after Stadler at The Belfry, the disease was obviously catching!

Once again, Faldo and Woosnam and Seve and Ollie, as Olazábal has now been affectionately known for many years, filled the bottom two slots and their play drew superlatives from their captain. 'Quite simply I have never seen such fantastic golf in foursome or fourball; it was just birdies all the way. In all the years I was captain, I never had as easy a time as I had at Muirfield Village in putting pairings together, as after the first series, those three pairs picked themselves.' That afternoon Faldo and Woosnam were 6 under par, beating Hal Sutton and Dan Pohl by 2/1, and the Spaniards went one better in defeating Curtis Strange and Tom Kite by a similar margin. For the first time Europe had won every single game in one series. It was Europe 6, the USA 2.

The following morning Brand and Rivero couldn't find the touch they had had the previous afternoon and lost, though their score of level par in foursomes is never bad. Faldo and Woosnam were a bit scruffy and lucky to halve, but behind them the golf was quite simply superb. Lyle and Langer gave the lie to the idea Lyle couldn't play foursomes, and were heading for a score in the mid-60s against Wadkins and Nelson, when they won on the 17th green.

The last game that morning again featured Ballesteros and Olazábal, now most comfortable in their anchor role, up against Crenshaw and Payne Stewart. A couple under par to the turn was good enough to give them a 3-hole lead, but things slipped a bit coming home and they were just 1 up on the 18th tee. The Americans were never going to do better than make five at the last. Even so, the two Spaniards – and Seve in particular – almost contrived to lose it. From a fine drive Seve found a greenside bunker; a deft recovery from Olazábal left his partner with a 7-foot downhill putt with two for the match. Seve knocked it 6 feet by! But Ollie saved the day and Europe were a further point in front from that morning's play.

Eamonn Darcy got his one outing before the singles that afternoon, replacing Rivero as Gordon Brand's partner, and for obvious reasons that was the only change in Jacklin's formidable line up. Faldo and Woosnam went first that afternoon and proceeded to birdie the first five holes and go to the turn in 29 – probably the best golf ever in the cauldron that is the Ryder Cup. Three more birdies followed and they were an approximate 10 under par when they shook hands on the 14th green. The Americans had done well to take the match that far!

But this wasn't all one-way traffic. In the second match, Bean and Stewart inflicted much the same pain on Brand and Darcy, also going out in 29. The two Europeans were entitled to feel aggrieved, being 5 under par when they lost by 3/2. Rough treatment, too, for Darcy, in his only game of the first two days. Sutton and Mize stood up well to the Spaniards, were 3 up at the turn and held on to win on the 17th green: one of the very few matches these two would lose in European colours during four battles for the Ryder Cup.

It was left to Langer and Lyle to tidy things up on that second afternoon. They were never down and, playing steadily rather than spectacularly, were 3 up and three to play, but had to go to the 18th to secure the win. In another first for Europe, they had tied or won each series of foursome and fourballs over those first two days: just one of many records Jacklin and his sides would garner over the eight years of his captaincy.

That extra point from the Saturday morning four-somes meant that Europe were now an extraordinary 5 points clear, leading the US 10½ to 5½, with just the singles to come. Only 3½ points were needed out of 12 to retain the trophy, but Jacklin and his men were after bigger things than that – a first ever win on American soil.

Singles has always been the Americans' strongest suit: being out there on their own and playing for them-selves is what they do best. Also, with all twelve players on both sides playing for the only time in the match, their greater strength in depth usually shines through. Time and again, over the next few years, Europe would establish a lead over the first couple of days and then struggle to hang on in the singles. In some ways it is almost as though having a lead – even though it may only be a point or two – places a burden of expectancy on the team, making victory that bit harder to achieve. If proof is needed, the only time the US got their noses in front after two days – in 1995 – they couldn't finish the job off either.

Surely, though, 5 points was an insuperable lead, yet it was to be a long hard day before the requisite points were on the board. It was fitting that Ian Woosnam should lead off the European challenge: he was atop the European Order of Merit, had won three tourna-ments that year, and would win another in Paris before the season was over. He liked to play quickly, and going out first could set his own pace. His opponent was the massive Andy Bean, a full foot taller than the Welshman. It was a dour rather than sparkling affair and Woosnam missed his chance when, 1 down and two to play and Bean in the scrub, he couldn't win the hole from the middle of the fairway. America had got the vital first point.

Howard Clark came next and neither he nor Sam Torrance had played since the first day. Both were near the top of Jacklin's singles line up. Clark's opponent, Dan Pohl, had also had Friday off, but had won a point the first morning. The golf in this match was not of the highest calibre, but Clark hung on to his man till the 18th, where Pohl made an awful mess. Clark, after a free drop from a camera position, was never going to take more than four and a doughty victory was his. That said, it was a game that was lost by the Americans rather than won by the Europeans. Above all it re-established Europe's 5-point advantage.

The 18th was also good to Torrance. His battle with Larry Mize was always close – never more than a hole in it – but Mize had the edge coming to the last. There he drove close to where Clark had had a free drop. However, Mize was just inside the line of a ditch running up the left side and his drop was under penalty. He still couldn't reach the green in three and now it was the Americans who were wilting at the end. That, though, is what the pressure of trying to come from behind does to you.

It was clear by now that every point was vital. Nick Faldo couldn't break free of Mark Calcavecchia and a couple of bogies coming home saw a narrow lead turn into loss by a single hole. Olazábal was never up on Payne Stewart, and bogies at both 16 and 18 gave the American that victory. What was now apparent – and would be in several of these contests in the years ahead – was if you had played in all four previous games on Friday and Saturday, precious little was left in the tank for Sunday. All Europe's big names were struggling, and Sandy Lyle soon became another casualty, losing to Tom Kite by 3/2.

For a long time it looked as though Bernhard Langer was heading down the same tube. After eleven holes he was 3 down to that great point-gatherer of former years, Larry Nelson. Nelson then made a mess of three holes in a row to let the German back in. Langer doesn't relinquish those sorts of chances and hung on well for a half.

Seve was looking comfortable against Curtis Strange, 3 up and six to play, and there was good news at the bottom, where Gordon Brand Jnr was 4 up through the turn against Hal Sutton. Both, though, began losing holes coming home and Europe started looking for someone, anyone, to bolster their wilting effort. It turned out to be the unlikely figure of Eamonn Darcy.

By the time Darcy teed his ball up in the singles at Muirfield Village, he was setting out on his eleventh individual match since his first outing in 1975 and was still looking for his first success. Be it foursomes, fourballs or singles, he had yet to win one. There had been a couple of halves along the way, but no victories. Against Crenshaw he was determined to put this right. After losing the 2nd hole, Darcy won four in a row from the 4th, three of them with birdies. More significantly, Crenshaw three-putted the 6th and then broke his putter by banging it on the ground. He couldn't mend it or replace it, and would have to finish the match holing out with one of the other thirteen in the bag. He chose a long iron for the long putts and the leading edge of his wedge for the short.

It turned out to have been the best thing Crenshaw could have done: he started holing putts. Three up to Darcy became 1 down and two to play. It was beginning to look as though Darcy would never experience the joy of winning a game in the Ryder Cup. But Crenshaw made a mess of the 17th and then drove into that ditch running up the left of 18. He dropped out under penalty and from the rough could only find a greenside bunker with his third. Darcy, from the middle of the fairway – and with the match at his mercy – put his approach in the same bunker.

Crenshaw came out to 10 feet, but below the hole, Darcy to 5 feet and above. On those lightening fast greens position was everything and any good golfer would have preferred Crenshaw's putt to that of Darcy, even though it was twice as far away. Needless to say, Crenshaw holed and by now, with things going wrong behind, it looked as though the whole match would hinge on Darcy's putt. Years later he could recall the moment and it still brought tears to his eyes: 'It was all downhill, and oh, so fast. I thought I could hole it, but if I didn't, I didn't think I would be able to get the one back; there would just be nothing to stop it. There was a little break from the left and I just kissed it, and in it went.'

With Langer's half-point, that meant the match could not be lost, and a moment or two later Seve shook hands with Strange on the 17th green to give Europe their first ever win against America, in America. It was somehow appropriate that a European – and who else but Seve – should have the honour, and against Nicklaus in his own backyard. After all, it was he who had suggested that Europeans be included all those years ago.

As for Tony Jacklin, what a triumph in three acts! In 1983 he had shown European golf what was possible if you gave your twelve best players the tools to do the job and the belief it could be done. Two years later, taking only the positives from that narrow defeat in Florida, he used it as a springboard to win the Cup for the first time in nearly 30 years. And two years after that, he bearded Jack Nicklaus in his own den and came away with the spoils. Jacklin had done with his teams what he had done as an individual – seen a challenge and gone for it, no matter what the odds.

In the aftermath of that great day in Ohio, with the cheers still echoing round the club, Ian Woosnam stood up and said what many were thinking: 'I'm not one for making speeches, but what this man has done today, he deserves a knighthood. And he's got to be captain again in 1989.' Two years earlier, Peter Jacobsen had said much the same at The Belfry: 'You should make Jacklin captain for the next 30 years; if not, you can send him over to us.' Twenty years later, Paul Azinger, on being asked at his own coronation as captain, who his vice-captains would be, said: 'to start with … probably Tony Jacklin.' That's how highly even his opponents rated his performance.

1989 – The Belfry

22–24 September

Europe (*Tony Jacklin*)	Matches		USA (*Ray Floyd*)

Foursomes: *Morning*

Europe			USA
N. Faldo & I. Woosnam (halved)	½	½	T. Kite & C. Strange (halved)
H. Clark & M. James	0	1	L. Wadkins & P. Stewart (1 hole)
S. Ballesteros & J.M. Olazábal (halved)	½	½	T. Watson & C. Beck (halved)
B. Langer & R. Rafferty	0	1	M. Calcavecchia & K. Green (2/1)

Fourballs: *Afternoon*

Europe			USA
S. Torrance & G. Brand Jnr (1 hole)	1	0	C. Strange & P. Azinger
H. Clark & M. James (3/2)	1	0	F. Couples & L. Wadkins
N. Faldo & I. Woosnam (2 holes)	1	0	M. Calcavecchia & M. McCumber
S. Ballesteros & J.M. Olazábal (6/5)	1	0	T. Watson & M. O'Meara

Foursomes: *Morning*

Europe			USA
I. Woosnam & N. Faldo (3/2)	1	0	L. Wadkins & P. Stewart
G. Brand Jnr & S. Torrance	0	1	C. Beck & P. Azinger (4/3)
C. O'Connor Jnr & R. Rafferty	0	1	M. Calcavecchia & K. Green (3/2)
S. Ballesteros & J.M. Olazábal (1 hole)	1	0	T. Kite & C. Strange

Fourballs: *Afternoon*

Europe			USA
N. Faldo & I. Woosnam	0	1	C. Beck & P. Azinger (2/1)
B. Langer & J.M. Canizares	0	1	T. Kite & M. McCumber (2/1)
H. Clark & M. James (1 hole)	1	0	P. Stewart & C. Strange
S. Ballesteros & J.M. Olazábal (4/2)	1	0	M. Calcavecchia & K. Green

Singles

Europe			USA
S. Ballesteros	0	1	P. Azinger (1 hole)
B. Langer	0	1	C. Beck (3/1)
J.M. Olazábal (1 hole)	1	0	P. Stewart
R. Rafferty (1 hole)	1	0	M. Calcavecchia
H. Clark	0	1	T. Kite (8/7)
M. James (3/2)	1	0	M. O'Meara
C. O'Connor Jnr (1 hole)	1	0	F. Couples
J.M. Canizares (1 hole)	1	0	K. Green
G. Brand Jnr	0	1	M. McCumber (1 hole)
S. Torrance	0	1	T. Watson (3/1)
N. Faldo	0	1	L. Wadkins (1 hole)
I. Woosnam	0	1	C. Strange (2 holes)

Europe	**14**	**14**	**USA**

Jacklin's instinct would surely have been to call it a day – nothing could match his achievements of the last five years, and any further involvement must inevitably be anti-climactic. However, there was a tremendous ground swell of enthusiasm for him to keep going. 'Already I am being asked whether I will be captain again,' was his comment a few weeks later. 'Of course it would be presumptuous of me to speculate; it is up to others to decide ... But if everyone who mattered was to suggest that they felt the best chance of another win was with me again, I would not shirk the responsibility.'

That was a door sufficiently ajar for 'everyone who mattered' to walk straight through. Yes, there really was little more to achieve, but if you are good at something then it's nice to carry on. After all, if you have won The Open Championship that doesn't mean you don't go on playing in it and trying to win it again.

Then, in the spring of the following year – scarcely six months after his great triumph in America – his wife Vivien tragically died: a brain haemorrhage while driving near their home in Spain. She was a great lady who had been a massive support to Tony throughout his golfing life and an enormous asset at his side during the stresses and strains of a Ryder Cup campaign. It was she who heard his desire for the wives to be part of his endeavour – an important element in creating that spirit of togetherness he believed so vital when trying to meld twelve strong characters into a team. This was her baton to pick up and run with.

First at The Belfry and later at Muirfield Village, the wives became a potent force – no flibbertigibbet bunch of WAGs these – not only within the team room, but out on the course as well. They did much to get the crowds up and behind the European side, and crowd support in both those matches – and in all the contests since, especially at home – has been a huge factor in helping lift the team to ever greater deeds. Time and again, and certainly during the years when, on paper, Europe was the lesser team, individuals performed seemingly better than their best and produced results above and beyond many people's hopes and expectations.

So another Ryder Cup would in some respects be cathartic for Tony Jacklin after his bereavement. He certainly wouldn't have wanted two huge holes in his life, and no Ryder Cup to think and worry about after the previous five years would have been another hole indeed. As it happened, he met another great lady, Astrid Waagen, whom he would marry at Christmas 1988, and she splendidly picked up the reins in both clothes design and team support.

The huge three-ring circus the Ryder Cup had now become might have fazed a shrinking violet, but to Astrid it was a variation on a theme she already knew well. She had previously been married to Alan Kendall, a guitarist with the Bee Gees, so the Ryder Cup was just a more refined version of what she'd experienced already. She had spent much of that life living in America, so knew what to lay on for the American wives when they came to Great Britain – a bit of the Bard at Stratford-upon-Avon and the best spa within easy reach. She also struck up what would be a lifelong friendship with Maria Floyd, her opposite number, and regardless of loyalties Maria was most helpful in showing her the ropes. Who said the Ryder Cup was all aggression and animosity?

So it was back to The Belfry for a second time. With his three picks, Jacklin was more than happy with the squad. Eamonn Darcy, Ken Brown and José Rivero had gone, to be replaced by Ronan Rafferty, who headed the Order of Merit that year, J.M. Canizares and Christy O'Connor Jnr. O'Connor Jnr who wasn't as close to automatic selection as he had been in 1985, but Tony picked him anyway and was well rewarded on the final day.

In Raymond Floyd, Jacklin had possibly the best opposite number he was to come up against. By now the Americans realised it was never again going to be just a case of turning up to win – you had to get in there and rattle the cage a little. And when you look at the calibre of individuals who made the American team, this was undoubtedly the best dozen Europe had come up against since Jacklin took over. This was not going to be any easier than the previous three.

Yet again, there was a poor European start in the foursomes the first morning: just two halved matches out of the four. Fortunately, the afternoon script followed past experience as well, Europe winning all four fourball matches, just as they had done two years earlier. With both foursomes and fourballs being shared on the Saturday, once again Europe had a 2-point lead ahead of the singles.

In the singles Jacklin went with his original idea of how his line up should be – putting power top and bottom, with the lesser lights tucked away in the middle. But in the event it was those middle-order batsmen who got him out of trouble. By now Ballesteros and Co. were into their thirties, and with a couple of Ryder Cup victories behind them, had a little less adrenaline in the system to see them through the hectic three days. Jacklin, however, never deviated from the belief that his big names – his major winners – were the ones to keep sending out into the fray. This time though, by the time they got to the singles, they were a spent force: no points on Sunday from Ballesteros, Langer, Faldo or Woosnam.

It was Olazábal and Ronan Rafferty who got things back on track after Seve and Langer had lost the two top games, both Europeans winning by the narrowest margin against Payne Stewart and Mark Calcavecchia. Stewart was the first of four Americans to drive into the water at 18 and lose matches they could have halved or won. Indeed, it was the cheers from the partisan crowd as one American after another found the water that, to some extent, fuelled the bad feeling that was to emerge at Kiawah Island two years later.

Only Mark James won impressively, seeing off Mark O'Meara 3/2, but that only compensated for the 8/7 thrashing his chum Howard Clark got at the hands of Tom Kite. Kite won another victory, a verbal one, an hour later, when Europe had secured enough points to guarantee at least a half, and BBC presenter Steve Ryder asked one question too many by suggesting this losing business was becoming a bit of a habit for the Americans. Kite replied they hadn't lost this one and there were still three matches that could all go America's way, which as it turned out they duly did.

Perhaps for the one and only time in his long stint as captain, Tony Jacklin let his guard down once a share of the spoils had been assured and he joined in the cheers and celebrations around the 18th green, believing, perhaps – as most did – that victory would be delivered soon enough. Still out were Sam Torrance, Nick Faldo and Ian Woosnam, but with no one seemingly interested in their efforts any more, the lost concentration and Watson, Wadkins and Strange managed to salvage some US pride, all winning matches, one of which

Europe should at least have halved. So the match ended 14 points apiece.

That was the end of the Jacklin era, but what a mark he had made. Not only had he destroyed the myth of American invincibility, he had done wonders for the morale and standing of the European Tour. He had been fortunate to have had a collection of world-class players on which to mount his challenge, but the Ryder Cup is about twelve players not four or five, and Jacklin was the one who really believed the Cup could be won. What's more, he got his successive teams to believe it as well. With Jacklin as captain there was no such thing as a 'good try', 'near but not quite'. He told the world he could win this thing and he took his players with him

What will be hard to measure is how large a part Jacklin's achievements played in the evolution of the Tour itself, but it has been considerable. The successes of his teams and those that followed have been the shop window for the Tour these past twenty years, and on the back of it sponsorships have been sold and standards all-round have been raised. Many people have contributed to the Tour, making it what it is today, but Jacklin's input may just have been the biggest of all.

CHAPTER FIVE

Gallacher's Turn

1991 and 1993
Bernard Gallacher

Taking on the Ryder Cup captaincy after Tony Jacklin's great run could easily have been seen as a poisoned chalice. Yes, a great honour, but how could anyone compete with all he had achieved, especially as the golden blocks on which those achievements were built – that handful of major winners that came out of nowhere and might never be replaced – were getting older and close to the time when they wouldn't be able to play competitively in every series? It would be hard enough just to match the deeds of the 1980s, let alone transcend them, and there was always the possibility, likelihood even, that under another captain Europe might sink back into the role of underdog. That was the task facing Bernard Gallacher in 1991.

A less well balanced man might have flinched at the impossibility of it all. The last club professional to be

1991– Kiawah Island
27–29 September

Europe (*Bernard Gallacher*)	Matches		USA (*Dave Stockton*)
Foursomes: *Morning*			
S. Ballesteros & J.M. Olazábal (2/1)	1	0	P. Azinger & C. Beck
B. Langer & M. James	0	1	R. Floyd & F. Couples (2/1)
D. Gilford & C. Montgomerie	0	1	L. Wadkins & H. Irwin (4/2)
N. Faldo & I. Woosnam	0	1	P. Stewart & M. Calcavecchia (1 hole)
Fourballs: *Afternoon*			
S. Torrance & D. Feherty (halved)	½	½	L. Wadkins & M. O'Meara (halved)
S. Ballesteros & J.M. Olazábal (2/1)	1	0	P. Azinger & C. Beck
S. Richardson & M. James (5/4)	1	0	C. Pavin & M. Calcavecchia
N. Faldo & I. Woosnam	0	1	R. Floyd & F. Couples (5/3)
Foursomes: *Morning*			
S. Torrance & D. Feherty	0	1	H. Irwin & L. Wadkins (4/2)
M. James & S. Richardson	0	1	M. Calcavecchia & P. Stewart (1 hole)
N. Faldo & D. Gilford	0	1	P. Azinger & M. O'Meara (7/6)
S. Ballesteros & J.M. Olazábal (3/2)	1	0	F. Couples & R. Floyd
Fourballs: *Afternoon*			
I. Woosnam & P. Broadhurst (2/1)	1	0	P. Azinger & H. Irwin
B. Langer & C. Montgomerie (2/1)	1	0	S. Pate & C. Pavin
M. James & S. Richardson (3/1)	1	0	L. Wadkins & W. Levi
S. Ballesteros & J.M. Olazábal (halved)	½	½	F. Couples & P. Stewart (halved)
Singles			
N. Faldo (2 holes)	1	0	R. Floyd
D. Feherty (2/1)	1	0	P. Stewart
C. Montgomerie (halved)	½	½	M. Calcavecchia (halved)
J.M. Olazábal	0	1	P. Azinger (2 holes)
S. Richardson	0	1	C. Pavin (2/1)
S. Ballesteros (3/2)	1	0	W. Levi
I. Woosnam	0	1	C. Beck (3/1)
P. Broadhurst (3/1)	1	0	M. O'Meara
S. Torrance	0	1	F. Couples (3/2)
M. James	0	1	L. Wadkins (3/2)
B. Langer (halved)	½	½	H. Irwin (halved)
D. Gilford (halved)*	½	½	S. Pate (halved)
Europe	14½	14½	**USA**

*Pate withdrawn at start of day

involved either as player or captain, the Ryder Cup was not the be all and end all of Bernard's existence. At the time of his appointment there were no other candidates for the job, at least none with his qualifications. He had played in eight matches between 1969 and 1981, and then been Jacklin's assistant for the following three: Gallacher had been an integral part of the matches for more than twenty years. No one would deny it was his turn.

Gallacher is insistent that he was only ever an assistant, never vice-captain: 'That was something we never had in those days, in fact I don't know where that came from. I was only there to help. I never attended team meetings, indeed never went in the team room. Tony and I would have a meeting in the mornings and anything logistic I would sort out for him, but as for pairings or tactics that was up to Tony and the players, I never got involved.'

So perhaps Gallacher was not quite as up to speed with the intricacies of Jacklin's style of captaincy as might have been suspected. Also, Jacklin, with his two major championships, had the authority and confidence to make decisions that the Nick Faldos and Seve Ballesteroses would accept without question. Gallacher was not such a black-and-white thinker, and without Jacklin's track record, had to get his ideas across through discussion and consensus.

Jacklin's captaincy had been inspirational. As with his own playing career, he never contemplated failure; victory was the only option – an attitude Seve Ballesteros was to adopt in spades when he became captain a few years later. Most importantly, both Jacklin and Ballesteros were able to convey that attitude to the players under their command. These are gifts given to very few, and Gallacher's captaincy was more organisational than inspirational: 'I was keen on doing the job, thought I could do it, and was qualified to do it', was his practical assessment. 'I certainly never applied for it; it's not a job you canvass for, at least not back then!' A twinkle in the eye at that – a reference to the modern trend of 'throwing your cap into the ring', as both Ian Woosnam and Nick Faldo have done more recently. In Gallacher's eyes, it is an honour bestowed, not a job applied for.

In some ways Gallacher's captaincy was a throwback to the years before Jacklin: back to the times when the bulk of our Ryder Cup sides were made up of club professionals – good players who enhanced their club takings with the meagre pickings from a few tournaments in Britain and the lightly sponsored Continental Championships. Like captains from the 1970s and before, it was a task to be fitted in around other parts of his business life. He was the professional at Wentworth Golf Club which meant playing with and teaching its members, managing a handful of assistants and looking after a considerable retail operation.

He inherited and continued most of Jacklin's initiatives: the pursuit of excellence, bolstered by the best of everything, travelling first class. 'Compared with times I played', Gallacher says, 'Tony introduced a more relaxed style of captaincy. The players didn't have to dress up for formal team dinners, as had been the case in my day. His first concern was always for the team, and to cut out anything that might interfere with the best possible preparation.' Obviously this was a much better way for the team to get ready for the match and I ensured the off course activities were kept to a minimum.

Gallacher, of course, inherited what was still a very good side. Sandy Lyle may have gone, but he had been replaced by José Maria Olazábal; and Olazábal and Ballesteros had already forged what will surely prove to be the most successful partnership in Ryder Cup history. And Gallacher still had Ian Woosnam, Nick Faldo and Bernhard Langer. But in 1991 the first two didn't perform as expected: 'Ian Woosnam was no. 1 in the World and Nick Faldo no. 2', recalls Gallacher. 'They had been successful together in both the last two matches. So, along with Seve and Ollie, we had two cast-in-stone partnerships. But Nick and Ian didn't gel, and it wasn't till later I found out they didn't really want to play together. By then they had lost two matches on the first day.

'Successful partnerships occur when one player is more assertive than the other, a sort of team leader if you like. In the past, Woosnam had looked up to Faldo, who made all the decisions; Nick always made the decisions! By 1991, Ian had won the Masters, was no. 1 in the world and instead of working together, they competed with one another.'

Also, with their respective positions in the golf world, it was a partnership everyone expected to succeed, so there would not be the same joy or excitement for them even were they to win. Quite simply, it was a pairing that had run its course, before the 1991 match had even begun.

Kiawah Island was not a great venue for any first-time captain. Originally the match had been scheduled for a course out in Palm Springs, but just a month or two beforehand it was realised that, with two series of matches on the first two days, full television coverage would mean the games going on well into the evening schedules on the all-important East Coast. Many golf tournaments played over in the western United States often finish at 3 or 4 PM in order not to run into major network evening broadcasts on the other side. With 36 holes to be played each of the first two days, such an early finish would not be possible.

Landmark – a golf course management and development company – had acquired the rights to that year's match, so they simply moved it to their prime East Coast location, Kiawah Island. The only trouble was that the Ocean Course there wasn't really ready. Exposed to the wild Atlantic winds and tides, construction had been set back a couple of times and it still had an unfinished look about it. Also, the course – right at the far end of Kiawah Island, some 15 miles from the main road – was seen as the secluded jewel in the island's crown, destined to be an exclusive haven for the most privileged. The clubhouse was little more than a locker room and bar on stilts, and nowhere near big enough to house all the paraphernalia associated with an event like the Ryder Cup. Even the teams had to make do with a large Portakabin each for all their needs – not exactly suitable accommodation for the private jet brigade.

There were other disadvantages for Gallacher's first Ryder Cup adventure as captain: 'The support we had at Muirfield Village had been tremendous; a shock for the Americans and a great boost for us. Unfortunately at Kiawah, Keith Prowse was in charge of travel and transport at the UK end, and just before the match, they went bust. They'd already taken all the money, but that was then tied up in the courts, so a lot of people couldn't go who had wanted to go. Keith Prowse had been responsible for chartering Concorde, and it was only because Johnnie Walker stepped in and paid for it, that we could go by Concorde.'

Even for those that did go, it was not a great experience. The nearest town with any hotels was Charleston, and that was the best part of an hour away; then you had to park near the main road and be bussed in the last 15 miles. The land at the far end of Kiawah was only fractionally above sea level, so the ground on which the course was laid out had to be built up several feet to guarantee its survival in that wild location; but this left large stretches below the level of the greens and fairways, leaving spectators unable to follow the action. It was a course designed to be played exclusively in buggies and the 'walks' from green to tee were enormous, none more so than the 900 yards between the 9th green and 10th tee!

So, compared to the last couple of matches our support was a bit muted. Also, for the first time since these matches became close, the Americans were definitely more competitive and cohesive. Dave Stockton was their captain and he realised a new approach was needed if recent trends were to be reversed: 'We had just lost six straight years, hadn't seen the Cup, probably forgotten what it looked like. So there was a sense of urgency. When Nicklaus lost at Muirfield Village it became apparent to me, and every captain after me, that if Nicklaus can lose on his own course then anybody can get beat. If you're going to be successful you're going to have to dot the Is and cross the Ts of this thing.

'I knew I had to get the team to bond. I did a number of things to try and ensure it wasn't just one or two individuals that were going to carry it. I worked on getting them all to have a whole team concept.

The first Gulf War was still going on, so there was a lot of pride in America at that time. That certainly brought the guys together. The old forage caps might have looked a bit aggressive, but it was the symbol of pride we all felt at that time.

'I got the Tour to play shoot-outs on Tuesdays at tournaments, not just the usual old practice rounds. At half a dozen events I was able to put various players together, see how they got on, what worked and what didn't. A couple of times we even had a Ryder Cup format, a little match if you like. There were about four of us who used to meet up and talk Ryder Cup stuff; that was Paul Azinger, Payne Stewart, Lanny Wadkins and myself. We talked strategy, psychology, different things like that, and when we got to Kiawah I felt the team was ready to play, to win. It still blows me away that Lanny is one of the ones that didn't win when it was his turn in 1995, because he understood what we were about.'

There was also a definite edge to the match in 1991, so different to the usual celebration of all that's good in the game of golf. Two years previously there had been all that cheering at The Belfry, as one American after another drove into the water at 18 on the final afternoon. The Americans, shocked at their failure to win back the Cup, were equally shocked by what they perceived as unsportsmanlike behaviour from the crowd. At Kiawah Island there was an aggressive side to America's image as the perfect host.

At the gala dinner, among all the pleasantries, was fifteen minutes of film footage from previous Ryder Cups: there was not a single shot of a European player in its entirety. The film focused on great American play, but was totally unrepresentative of recent contests. It was, of course, put together by the TV company that had the rights, and if you have ever watched American coverage of any international contest, from the Olympics downwards, you hardly ever see any action from foreign nationals! So biased was it that one or two European dignitaries left early, and Jim Awtry of the US Professional Golfers Association did have the grace to apologise.

One other incident marred the otherwise smooth rhythm of the week. On the way to that dinner, the American motorcade suffered a crash and Steve Pate – arguably one of their stronger players at the time – was hurt, putting him out of action till the second series of fourballs. Having played without apparent discomfort, Pate was suddenly withdrawn overnight from the singles after losing. The first Gallacher knew was when he saw the draw over breakfast on the Sunday morning, Stockton not having had the courtesy to contact him and let him know.

'Pate had been drawn to play Seve,' recalls Gallacher, 'and that week Seve was going to beat whoever he played. By the nature of how those things work out, the draw shifted down and Seve was left against Wayne Levi, who anyone on our side would have beaten; he'd only had one game, and lost that.' Gallacher would never call foul play, but the incident reduced the potency of the European effort, and the Americans gained half a point that even a fit Steve Pate would probably not have achieved.

Ballesteros had long been the on-the-course inspiration of European teams; Jacklin had almost christened him his playing captain, and by elevating him to first among equals and seeking his opinion on all playing matters, had got the Spaniard's undying enthusiasm for the cause: 'Seve was great during the practice rounds', Gallacher remembers, 'he insisted in having a game with all the rookies, taking them under his wing, telling them all the little secrets to coping with the pressures, on and off the course; he even tried to transplant some of his miraculous short game into those less gifted. You didn't get that from Nick, he was more wrapped up in his own game, but from Nick you got points.' But there were no points from Faldo in 1991 until the singles.

Gallacher had long written down two banker pairings for both foursomes and fourballs. Faldo and Woosnam, Seve and Ollie, but only the Spaniards delivered. There was one other partnership that looked competitive, Bernhard Langer and Mark James: 'Mark was one of my picks, because he had a good foursomes and four-ball record, had won with lots of different partners', said Gallacher. 'The first morning is time for experience to get things rolling, so we had all our old hands out.'

One pairing that didn't come into that category was David Gilford and Colin Montgomerie, both first timers: 'They really forced themselves into consideration by playing so well in practice', was Gallacher's reason for putting them out together. 'They had similar types of games, hit all the fairways and greens, ideal for foursomes you'd think.' An inspirational pairing had it worked; on this occasion it didn't. Up against the old warhorses, Lanny Wadkins and Hale Irwin, they were soon swept away by the pressures of the first morning of a Ryder Cup and the competitive competence of their opponents.

Indeed, for much of that first set of foursomes things didn't go well anywhere. Langer and James were fighting a close but losing battle against Fred Couples and Ray Floyd (Floyd had been the US captain two years previously, usually a sign your days of playing in the match are over!) Gilford and Monty were never up, and even the talismanic pairing of Seve and Ollie were quickly 3 down to Paul Azinger and Chip Beck. At that stage only Faldo and Woosnam seemed fully engaged, out last against Payne Stewart and Mark Calcavecchia. As Gallacher was to later reflect, this was a very good American side, and Stockton had also started with his best and most experienced players.

Prior to all these matches, there is always an in-depth rules meeting between officials and all members of both teams. This is partly because matchplay – particularly in fourball and foursome – is rarely played by professionals these days. Also, both US and European Tours have their own set of rules to deal with tournament oddities such as temporary immovable obstructions or where to drop the ball – a whole set of minutiae special to the tournament professional. And these rules differ slightly from one tour to another.

What would be touched on, but is absolutely standard in all forms of golf, pro or amateur, is that whatever type of ball you tee off with in foursomes, both players will play that ball throughout. Obviously, tournament professionals each have their own preferred make and compression of ball, and one of the first things any new partnership will do is agree which ball they will use, meaning one or other will probably have to give up his own choice. Indeed, pairings have been known to emerge simply because both parties play the same ball. Azinger and Beck would have been well aware of what was right or wrong, yet on the 7th tee of the match against Seve and Ollie, they switched from 90 compression to 100, and did the same thing a couple of holes later. Of course, all top players will go through several balls during a competition round and it is quite possible, in the heat of battle, to reach for a new ball on any given tee, forgetting the nicety of the rule in operation for the Ryder Cup.

Another rule of golf is that any infringement in matchplay must be resolved before driving off the next tee. When this subject was being debated on the 10th tee, with both captains involved, there was just a hint that Seve felt all the last three holes might be coming his way as the infringements started on the 7th! It was sorted out, though, with just the loss of the 9th for the Americans.

But the Americans' rhythm had been broken, the Spaniards found their form, and a losing match was turned round. It was to be the first of three consecutive wins for these two – an achievement that was to keep Europe in the competition, as very little went right elsewhere. Faldo and Woosnam lost at the 18th and did so again after lunch in what was to be their last outing together.

There were some bright stories, however, Woosnam joining Paul Broadhurst to win a fourball on the second afternoon, and Mark James found a successful partnership with Steven Richardson to win twice; Montgomerie won with Langer on day two – an ideal partnership, which would keep reappearing from time to time right up to 2002, when Langer would play in his last Ryder Cup.

However, Faldo's form was cause for concern: 'He was playing all right when he arrived, hitting the ball very well, but like most of the team found the new strain of grass on the greens, Tiftdwarf, difficult to read', recalls Gallacher. 'He couldn't hole a putt for love nor money. He let it affect the rest of his game. By now I realised what I should have known from the start. He and Woosie no longer wanted to play together. I thought to give Nick some responsibility for shepherding one of the newcomers. I still felt David Gilford was basically playing well; his game was ideal for foursomes, so sent the pair of them out on the second morning. It was a disaster. Nick was by now so deep inside his own shell, he never made any effort to communicate with his partner, let alone help him through the rigours of a Ryder Cup. That was another bit of inspiration that went wrong!

'If I have any anxiety over that first Ryder Cup, it is for David Gilford. In hindsight two rookies going out on the first morning is not a good thing. Obviously putting him with Faldo was a mistake, and then there was the issue of the brown envelope.' (In the Ryder Cup, when it comes to the singles and every player is involved, each captain puts the name of one player in the 'brown envelope' – the man who would not play in the event that one of the other side could not play due to ill health.)

'I had put David's name in the envelope because he had played twice and lost twice, but never thought it would be used. In all the years I had played, and the years of Tony's captaincy, the brown envelope had never been an issue and who was in it never discussed or divulged. Steve Pate had played the second afternoon, so the thought he might not play never entered my mind.

'Again, one of the failings of Kiawah as a venue was we had no team room back at the hotel; some had breakfast there, some at the course. When I saw the draw, and that Stockton had pulled Pate out, David was already on his way out there, and it was Tony Jacklin who gave him the news. I certainly should have been there for that and felt really bad about it.

'Perhaps the one thing I did get right was to put Nick Faldo out top in the singles. In the frame of mind he was in, had I put him in the middle of the pack, he would just have gone on introspectively and probably lost. As it was, I felt his pride wouldn't let him lose at number one; he'd be in the limelight and he'd concentrate on the match, not worrying about what was wrong with his game. As it turned out, that was exactly what happened, and the golf in that top game with Ray Floyd was the best played that day.'

After the foursomes and fourballs and with the match tied at 8 points apiece, Nick Faldo and David Feherty, playing at numbers one and two, gave Europe a winning start. Very quickly Azinger and Corey Pavin got the Americans back on even terms. Montgomerie then started his Ryder Cup singles career with an astonishing half; at one point 5 down, and then still 4 down and four to play, his opponent Mark Calcavecchia imploded over the last few holes. Despite this amazing collapse, the US still seemed destined for their usual triumph in the singles.

Beck, Wadkins and Couples all won with a bit in hand, and it looked like the finishing touches would soon be provided by Hale Irwin, 2 up and four to play against Bernhard Langer. Langer had to win for Europe to tie and so retain the trophy. Now neither Langer nor Irwin is the swiftest in the world and it was an agonising hour with Europe's hopes hanging on every shot, every putt. Langer holed from 6 feet to win the 15th, got up and down from a bunker at 16 for a half there, holed another good putt to win 17, and then found the fairway at 18. Even Irwin, the winner of three US Opens was in shock.

Irwin definitely pulled his drive at 18, perhaps 30 to 40 yards left of the intended line. To this day no one knows how much if any it was kept in play by the dense crowd, but, though short, it was on the edge of the fairway, too far back to go for the green. The pin was in a most inaccessible spot and with Irwin unlikely to make four, Langer played for the middle of the green, pushed it a bit and it finished some 20 yards away. Irwin duly took five; Langer's approach putt ended some 6 feet past – it was this for a win and to tie the match.

The memory of Langer's putt is etched on the minds of all who saw it, as it is on Langer's: 'The line of the putt was the left edge of the hole. Pete Colman [Langer's caddy] pointed to a pair of spike marks right on that line, and they weren't so little. I was sure if I hit it at them the ball might go anywhere. So we determined it might be better to putt it straight and hope it wouldn't break too much. I made a pretty good stroke, but it did break too much and the ball went right over the side of the hole.

'I was shocked, sad for the team, but didn't feel I had let anyone down. I had made a good stroke and the ball hadn't gone in. Faced with the same situation, I would probably have made the same decision. I didn't mention the spike marks for some time as I felt it might sound like an excuse, that I'd yipped it or something. But the truth came out in time.'

In truth, it was a match in which Europe had been on

the back foot for much of the three days, and a tie would not really have been a true reflection of the pattern of the match. Looking back, Dave Stockton was the first, and so far the last, US captain to really get to grips with the intricacies of captaincy and try and understand what is required to meld a cohesive unit out of twelve talented individuals. He never even got a second go, nor has anyone tried to follow his hands-on example – that is, until his very good friend Paul Azinger got the captaincy for 2008.

1993 – The Belfry
24–26 September

Europe (*Bernard Gallacher*)	Matches		USA (*Tom Watson*)
Foursomes: *Morning*			
S. Torrance & M. James	0	1	L. Wadkins & C. Pavin (4/3)
I. Woosnam & B. Langer (7/5)	1	0	P. Azinger & P. Stewart
S. Ballesteros & J.M. Olazábal	0	1	T. Kite & D. Love III (2/1)
N. Faldo & C. Montgomerie (4/3)	1	0	R. Floyd & F. Couples
Fourballs: *Afternoon*			
I. Woosnam & P. Bakes (1 hole)	1	0	J. Gallagher Jnr & L. Janzen
B. Langer & B. Lane	0	1	L. Wadkins & C. Pavin (4/2)
N. Faldo & C. Montgomerie (halved)	½	½	P. Azinger & F. Couples (halved)
S. Ballesteros & J.M. Olazábal (4/3)	1	0	D. Love III & T. Kite
Foursomes: *Morning*			
N. Faldo & C. Montgomerie (3/2)	1	0	L. Wadkins & C. Pavin
B. Langer & I. Woosnam (2/1)	1	0	F. Couples & P. Azinger
P. Baker & B. Lane	0	1	R. Floyd & P. Stewart (3/2)
S. Ballesteros & J.M. Olazábal (2/1)	1	0	D. Love III & T. Kite
Fourballs: *Afternoon*			
N. Faldo & C. Montgomerie	0	1	J. Cook & C. Beck (2 holes)
M. James & C. Rocca	0	1	C. Pavin & J. Gallacher Jnr (5/4)
I. Woosnam & P. Baker (6/5)	1	0	F. Couples & P. Azinger
J.M. Olazábal & J. Haeggman	0	1	R. Floyd & P. Stewart (2/1)
Singles			
I. Woosnam (halved)	½	½	F. Couples (halved)
B. Lane	0	1	C. Beck (1 hole)
C. Montgomerie (1 hole)	1	0	L. Janzen
P. Baker (2 holes)	1	0	C. Pavin
J. Haeggman (1 hole)	1	0	J. Cook
M. James	0	1	P. Stewart (3/2)
C. Rocca	0	1	D. Love III (1 hole)
S. Ballesteros	0	1	J. Gallacher Jnr (3/2)
J.M. Olazábal	0	1	R. Floyd (2 holes)
B. Langer	0	1	T. Kite (5/3)
N. Faldo (halved)	½	½	P. Azinger (halved)
S. Torrance (halved)*	½	½	L. Wadkins (halved)
Europe	**13**	**15**	**USA**

*Torrance withdrawn at start of day

'The one thing I learned from Kiawah Island was to think more deeply about the pairings, talk more to the players about who they would like to play with, even who they wouldn't want to play with. I still had Seve and Ollie, who never imagined they wouldn't be playing together. Other than that I still had a great side, we were back at The Belfry, a tried and tested venue, where we were guaranteed great support, where everything was sure to work well.'

Bernard Gallacher was confident in 1993. Kiawah Island had been difficult, but it had been a great match, right up there with those historic contests of the 1980s, and but for a missed 5-foot putt at the very end, the trophy would still be in Europe's hands.

One of the great partnerships of the 1980s, Faldo and Woosnam, may have gone, but it had been replaced almost immediately with another that looked every bit as good. Long before the teams arrived at The Belfry, the talk had been of Colin Montgomerie being the perfect partner for Nick Faldo, and so it proved. It certainly met Gallacher's criterion of any successful partnership requiring one assertive player and one happy to play the minor role. Monty was only in his second Ryder Cup, Kiawah Island not having been an unqualified success from his point of view, and still a year or so short of the start of his European domination.

Mind you, being Faldo's partner is not a bed of roses. It's one thing to have the senior man making all the decisions, but with Faldo, you have to play the game his way as well, sometimes to an unbelievable extent. It is now a matter of record that Monty is a far superior putter in the Ryder Cup than he is day in day out on Tour. But back then, Faldo had his own putting routine and he insisted Monty went along with it: 'It started in the practice rounds,' recalls Montgomerie, 'I would look at a putt and think it was right or left lip, but Nick would say that was far too casual, and between us, particularly in foursomes, we would have to work out the four or five points over which the ball had to travel to get to the hole; sort of golfing dot-to-dot, you might say.'

There were one or two worries for Gallacher though: 'Bernhard Langer came into the match not having played for six weeks; he'd had a neck injury. It was ok, but he was short of match practice and five rounds in three days was going to be a lot to ask of someone not fully fit. Then there was Ballesteros. He'd had a very poor year and I had had to give him a captain's pick; back then a side without Seve was unthinkable and with four out of the five series fourballs or foursomes, he was a vital part of that great partnership with Olazábal. Because of his poor form, what I didn't get from him that year was his work with the rookies, his captain's role on the course; he was too wrapped up in trying to sort out his own game.'

For a day and a half, all went well. Faldo and Monty clocked up 2½ points out of 3, Seve and Ollie – despite a hiccough on the first morning, and clearly neither of them playing anywhere near their best – won twice. A new partnership of Ian Woosnam and Bernhard Langer contributed a couple of foursomes' points: in fact, Woosnam got 4 points out of 4 those first two days, as he successfully teamed up with Peter Baker in the four-balls. But it was still the old soldiers, the great players from the 1980s, that were producing the points, and, looking to the future, there was going to come a time when they would no longer be around.

However, on a sunny Saturday morning, all seemed to be going well. Indeed, Europe were heading for 3 points out of 4 and a 3-point lead, with the afternoon fourballs still to come. 'I was beginning to think about winning the Ryder Cup that Saturday afternoon,' recalls Gallacher, 'then at 11.45 I got word that Seve wanted to see me on the 14th fairway. He was in the bottom foursome and he and Ollie were 2 up. He knew I had to have the afternoon pairings in at 12.00, but he wanted to say he didn't want to play that afternoon. "But you're 2 up, you're going to win again and this partnership can always get points," I told him. But he was adamant, he was dragging Olazábal down, his own play was too poor and he wanted to work on the practice ground to be ready to play in the singles. He wouldn't change his mind.

'Moments later, Langer called in to say he wouldn't be able to play in the afternoon; his neck was too sore, and he wanted to rest to be ready for the singles. So with just a few minutes to go, I had to split up two winning partnerships and put two new pairings together, with little or no warning.'

Two rookies came off the bench, Costantino Rocca and captain's pick Joakim Haeggman, but to no avail. The momentum had swung to the Americans and they won the afternoon fourballs 3–1. What should have been a commanding lead going into the singles was a nail-biting 1 point. Most disappointing was a lacklustre performance from Faldo and Montgomerie. Playing a couple of less well-known Americans, John Cook and Chip Beck, it was one of those games they were expected to win, with not a lot of glory even if they did.

There was a chance right at the end when, 1 down and one to play, Faldo hit his approach to 18 some 10 feet from the pin, while the Americans both ended up some 18 yards away. Now the rules of fourballs state that either member of a team with a player furthest from the hole can play. Often this means the man nearest to the hole can hole out (perhaps to get the half and so give his partner a 'free' putt for the win) before either of the opponents can putt. With Monty furthest away, and no longer in the hole, this was an option. However, for those who know and play a lot of fourball matches, this most certainly was not one of those moments. Even if Faldo holed out, their opponents knew that they would have to hole to win the match and they would not, therefore, have to worry about the one back. Miss it and it's all over. The sensible option would have been to let the Americans play first – they have to make certain they don't both three-putt. In other words, there is doubt. But no, Faldo went first, missed and that was that. Much of the good work of the first day and a half had come undone.

What had looked a good thing halfway through Saturday was now looking distinctly doubtful. There were mutterings that Tony Jacklin would never have allowed Seve and Langer to excuse themselves from that afternoon's play, and maybe the results would have been different. Hindsight makes experts of us all. Of concern going into that Sunday was the form of Ballesteros and Langer's health; and Gallacher had another problem too. Sam Torrance, one of Europe's stronger players, had been a passenger from the beginning. He'd had a bad toe for a week or two, but instead of getting better, it became infected, and after one go in the first set of foursomes, he had been unable to play: 'He could just about have played in the singles,' Gallacher feels, 'but it would have meant him having a painkilling injection before the start and another at the turn. He hadn't played since Friday morning, it wasn't getting any better, and you honestly couldn't say he was fit to play. The name in the little brown envelope was meant for just such an occasion.'

The Americans would have known there was a strong likelihood Torrance wouldn't be able to play, and that the brown envelope would be needed. Rather than leave captain Tom Watson with the invidious task of selecting someone to sit out, Lanny Wadkins, with the best ever American record behind him, put his hand up and Watson accepted. Certainly it saved him from making that awkward decision, but to have just about your best competitor settling for half a point, with the match so close, must have made Watson think for a moment or two.

Both at Kiawah Island and The Belfry, Gallacher followed tradition in his singles draw: 'I like the team to have a balanced look about it for the singles, with some strength at the top, a bit in the middle and some old hands down the bottom, should it get tight.' No change from Jacklin there. The Americans, apart from putting Fred Couples out top, put most of their firepower down the bottom. A look at the draw, and with the fitness and form problems the European team was carrying, the US now looked favourites.

Europe made a bright start. Ian Woosnam had the first of his three singles matches against Fred Couples and got a half. Then Montgomerie, Baker and Haeggmann all put points on the board. Indeed, well into the afternoon, things looked bright for Europe as Barry Lane in match two was 3 up and five to play against Chip Beck; were he to win, that would have been 4½ points from the first five games. But that lead slipped away and what had looked a certain point went the other way. Costantino Rocca also looked to be on his way to victory, 1 up and two to play against Davis Love. He was on the green in two at the par-5 17th, with his opponent some way short. A 2/1 win looked most likely but Love pitched to a few feet. Rocca misjudged his approach putt, knocked it 6 feet past and missed the return. Love holed, squared the game and then won the last as well. With Lane's loss to Beck, that was two unlikely points to the Americans and the turning point of the entire match.

A debilitated Europe could not survive two such blows. Seve, Olazábal and Langer, despite two of them having had the previous afternoon off, never got into their matches and all too soon the Americans had won another series of singles and with it the Trophy. Even a hole-in-one by Faldo at the 14th, in the bottom match against Paul Azinger, counted for nought, as by then the overall match was over and the pair agreed a half.

A narrow loss at Kiawah Island was acceptable – there was much about that venue that made it a most difficult away match. Here though, Europe were at what had become almost the spiritual home of the Ryder Cup and there had been the usual great support from the home crowd, yet victory had once again slipped through their fingers.

Gallacher was beginning to be seen as an unlucky captain. He hadn't done much wrong, but luck had conspired against him. Normally that would be that; two goes was the most anyone had had unless they had been inordinately successful, such as Tony Jacklin or before him, Dai Rees. The Fates, however, would decree otherwise.

Oak Hill

22–24 September

Europe (*Bernard Gallacher*)	Matches		USA (*Lanny Wadkins*)
Foursomes: *Morning*			
N. Faldo & C. Montgomerie	0	1	C. Pavin & T. Lehman (1 hole)
S. Torrance & C. Rocca (3/2)	1	0	J. Haas & F. Couples
H. Clark & M. James	0	1	D. Love III & J. Maggert (4/3)
B. Langer & P.-U. Johansson (1 hole)	1	0	B. Crenshaw & C. Strange
Fourballs: *Afternoon*			
D. Gilford & S. Ballesteros (4/3)	1	0	B. Faxon & P. Jacobsen
S. Torrance & C. Rocca	0	1	J. Maggert & L. Roberts (6/5)
N. Faldo & C. Montgomerie	0	1	F. Couples & D. Love III (3/2)
B. Langer & P.-U. Johansson	0	1	C. Pavin & P. Mickelson (6/4)
Foursomes: *Morning*			
N. Faldo & C. Montgomerie (4/2)	1	0	C. Strange & J. Haas
S. Torrance & C. Rocca (6/5)	1	0	D. Love III & J. Maggert
I. Woosnam & P. Walton	0	1	L. Roberts & P. Jacobsen (1 hole)
B. Langer & D. Gilford (4/3)	1	0	C. Pavin & T. Lehman
Fourballs: *Afternoon*			
S. Torrance & C. Montgomerie	0	1	B. Faxon & F. Couples (4/2)
I. Woosnam & C. Rocca (3/2)	1	0	D. Love III & B. Crenshaw
S. Ballesteros & D. Gilford	0	1	J. Haas & P. Mickelson (3/2)
N. Faldo & B. Langer	0	1	C. Pavin & L. Roberts (1 hole)
Singles			
S. Ballesteros	0	1	T. Lehman (4/3)
H. Clark (1 hole)	1	0	P. Jacobsen
M. James (4/3)	1	0	J. Maggert
I. Woosnam (halved)	½	½	F. Couples (halved)
C. Rocca	0	1	D. Love III (3/2)
D. Gilford (1 hole)	1	0	B. Faxon
C. Montgomerie (3/1)	1	0	B. Crenshaw
N. Faldo (1 hole)	1	0	C. Strange
S. Torrance (2/1)	1	0	L. Roberts
B. Langer	0	1	C. Pavin (3/2)
P. Walton (1 hole)	1	0	J. Haas
P.-U. Johansson	0	1	P. Mickelson (2/1)
Europe	14½	13½	**USA**

CHAPTER SIX

Gallacher's Last Chance

1995
Bernard Gallacher

After two defeats you would have thought it was time for someone else to have a go at the captaincy; indeed, that Bernard Gallacher might have had enough. He had had a couple of good tries, but not quite able to generate the passion and enthusiasm that gave so much power to Tony Jacklin's campaigns. But in 1995 it was going to be difficult for anyone else to fill the role.

By now it was generally assumed that Seve Ballesteros would be captain at Valderama two years hence. In 1995, and as yet under 40, he still had ambitions to play, still dreamt that it was only a matter of time before his glorious best returned and that further deeds of der-ring-do awaited in Ryder Cups and elsewhere. He might still even be a player in 1997, but Seve and the European Tour would tackle the tricky question of him handling the by now impossible task of being both

Captain and player, as and when that issue arose.

So whoever captained the side in 1995 would be a one-off. There was still no obvious candidate to replace Gallacher. The big guns were still firing – just – and the best of the other regular players during the 1980s were still performing. Sandy Lyle had departed the scene, but was campaigning in America – somewhat out of sight and out of mind. Peter Oosterhuis, perhaps the best of those from the pre-Jacklin years, was also permanently in the States and never really considered. So eventually the Ryder Cup committee turned to Gallacher one last time.

Perhaps surprisingly, he was happy to have another go: 'Before I ever started, I made up my mind to enjoy it, and I had done. I always, as a player, enjoyed Ryder Cups, the camaraderie, the forming of partnerships, friendships, and I found the same as captain. I never found it stressful, like Sam Torrance or Seve did. I'm not as emotional as those guys – Sam, Seve and Tony Jacklin. I tried to keep the pressure to the golf course, and not to still have it around off the course. I tried to instil that in the players.'

He certainly hadn't done badly in his two previous attempts, having overcome some considerable hurdles. Perhaps Jacklin might have snatched victory from one or even both of those close contests – who knows? And by now Gallacher had considerable experience in the job. Anyway, off he went, back to the States for one last try.

If Gallacher did have a weakness, it was a lack of intuition as to what might – or, more specifically, might not – work as pairings and partnerships. This was most apparent in 1991 with the failure of Nick Faldo and Ian Woosnam to achieve under Gallacher what they had for

Tony Jacklin. Gallacher never quite saw when such a tie-up had run its course, when there was, in a sense, nothing left to play for, no excitement in a pairing. He made the same mistake again in 1995 with Faldo and Colin Montgomerie: 'Nick still wanted to play with Colin Montgomerie, and with his record he could usually have what he wanted', was Gallacher's justification for once more putting together the successful pairing from 1993. He still saw it as a senior/junior partnership: 'Monty was still happy to go along with what Nick wanted. This was not a competing relationship as Faldo/Woosnam had become by 1991.'

But the dynamics had changed. Montgomerie was now into his phenomenal run as the top player in Europe – a position he would hold for another seven years. Faldo had not played enough in Europe – nor done well enough when he had – to qualify as of right for the team: he'd had to have one of Gallacher's wild-cards. It was three years since his last major victory, at The Open of 1992, and though he would win the Masters the following spring, his powers were definitely on the wane. Yet he still demanded the right to make the decisions, demanded the game be played his way. Of course he wanted to play with Monty, who wouldn't? However, Monty was by now the best player on the team and was to become the talisman of all those victories over the decade that lay ahead. He was ready for bigger things than playing number 2 to Nick Faldo.

It was a partnership that had run its course. As golfers they were different in almost every way. Faldo with his man-made swing, engineered to produce flawless golf, and Montgomerie just swinging the way he always had, seemingly never having to think how to do it, just aiming in the right direction. They were never natural golfing buddies and sure enough it didn't work. They lost both matches the first day, won a solitary foursomes the second morning, and by then Gallacher had to split them anyway to try to get 2 points in the afternoon fourballs from what were arguably his two best players. He didn't get any.

All that, of course, came once the match had got underway. Prior to that, Gallacher had another raft of problems to cope with. Just as the team was about to board Concorde for the flight to America, the press broke a story concerning Nick Faldo's marriage problems. He had been playing almost exclusively in America, basing himself in Orlando, while wife Gill was back in England bringing up the children. That summer he had formed the relationship that was to bring their marriage to an end. Faldo wasn't on Concorde, he was already in America. Gill, being completely in the dark until the news broke, travelled with the team, but in floods of tears. Faldo greeted the team as it came off Concorde, embraced some of the wives and girlfriends, and shook his wife by the hand. It didn't get any better: 'It is amazing how well Nick played, considering what was going on in his private life,' reflects Gallacher, 'Gill and Lesley [Bernard's wife] are best friends and neither of them knew what was going on until it broke in the press just as we were leaving.'

Then there had been the ailments of José Maria Olazábal. Although coming to an end, we were still in the era when the big four or five won most of the points, so there was always great public concern regarding the quality of the European team; there was still the perception we couldn't be really competitive, especially over there in the States, without the best possible line-up.

That summer, Olazábal started to suffer with back and foot problems – pictures of him hobbling up the steps from the 18th green at Riviera in the US PGA that August are still vivid. He was one of Gallacher's wild-cards, another, like Faldo, who played mostly in the US and because of the onset of his health crisis had not got enough points back home to qualify. Hoping for a miracle, Ollie was given till the last minute to get himself fit. It was not to be, and the Spaniard was out of the game for the best part of two years.

Olazábal's withdrawal from the team wasn't all bad news. Ian Woosnam hadn't had a good enough year to qualify as of right and Gallacher's initial problem was the need to pick two from Faldo, Woosnam and Olazábal. Woosnam had been the one to miss out. When Ollie had to pull out, Gallacher had Woosnam to fall back on.

Also on the plus side, this time Europe did not have a great US team to play against. Those doughty old war horses, Ray Floyd and Lanny Wadkins, had hung up their competitive boots, Wadkins becoming captain. Paul Azinger wasn't there either, diagnosed with cancer soon after his PGA Championship victory in 1993, and Payne Stewart and Tom Kite didn't make the team. In their place was Peter Jacobsen, who'd already flirted with giving up playing the game for commentary, Ben Crenshaw, way past his best and only on the team as a result of his emotional win at Augusta that year, a win he dedicated to his late coach Harvey Penick, Jeff Maggert, a competent journeyman but unlikely to frighten anyone and Brad Faxon, whose well known waywardness off the tee was likely to be found out on the tight tree-lined fairways of Oak Hill.

Wadkins then appeared to compound the team's

problems by plucking Curtis Strange from the lower reaches of the US money list as one of his wildcards, on account of his 'heart and guts'. But as one journalist put it: 'heart and guts aren't much good if you've already lost by 4/3'. Strange would play three matches and lose the lot. Against this Wadkins did have one of the best competitors ever to don US colours in the then US Open Champion Corey Pavin; and for the first time Phil Mickelson was in the side. Mickelson has always been an erratic driver and he, too, didn't play either foursome, but would still win 3 points out of 3.

If Mickelson and Faxon had trouble finding the fairways off the tee, Seve Ballesteros couldn't keep his drives in New York State. He had had quite a good year, including his last ever European Tour title, the Spanish Open in Madrid, and comfortably played his way into the side. But his form had deteriorated alarmingly in the second half of the year and he arrived in the US with no idea how to keep the ball in play. With all his driving problems, he had steadfastly refused to contemplate an iron off the tee or try to find a safe fade – a stock shot – just to give himself a chance. Even had Olazábal been fit, their great partnership would have come to its inevitable end at Oak Hill. At least they went out on a winning note at The Belfry in 1993, having by then won eleven matches together, lost two and halved two: a record surely no other pair will ever get near.

So Gallacher almost had to make a fresh start with his pairings, and perhaps one reason for sticking with Faldo and Montgomerie was that at least it gave a semblance of continuity, of substance, to his first morning's line-up. It was something for the rest, going out with new partners, to look at and feel reassured by: 'I wasn't totally without established pairings', recalls Gallacher,

'I had Bernhard Langer and Ian Woosnam, who had played well together two years previously, winning twice in foursomes, and I intended putting them together again. Then I was going to put Philip Walton out with Sam Torrance, as both of them were taught by Sam's dad, Bob Torrance, and knew one another well.' Putting a rookie out with an old hand is always sound practice but even this game plan came unstuck: 'In the practice rounds Philip's game began to go off, and I asked him if he was still happy about opening up in the first set of foursomes. He said he wasn't really ready and would prefer to wait till the fourballs. No sooner that, than Ian came to me and said he didn't want to play tomorrow, "You know, my game's not really there," he said, and of course he hadn't had a good year having been 13th choice.

'Now all this came up in the final practice,' mused Gallacher. 'I always insist that the final nine holes of practice be played as strict foursomes, no second shots, so we would all go into the first morning in foursome mode. Now I really was starting from scratch, and I ended up putting Langer with Per-Ulrik Johansson, and Sam Torrance with Costantino Rocca. I'd thought of Langer and Johansson as a possible pairing, fourballs perhaps, but Torrance and Rocca; where that came from I've no idea! And they both came off!'

But that's all that worked that first morning. With no spark, Faldo and Montgomerie were done on the last green by Corey Pavin and Tom Lehman. Meanwhile, Howard Clark and Mark James were well dusted by Davis Love III and Jeff Maggert: 'At that point I told Howard and Mark I wanted them to prepare themselves for the singles; that they had a big job to do for the team,' says Gallacher. 'I didn't want them out there doing all this supporting the team stuff, I wanted them out playing behind the matches each day and getting ready for the singles.' Something else a little hard to fathom, but it would work on the day.

'Then I made my one real mistake', laughs Gallacher. 'I had one or two other pairings for the fourballs that afternoon, but as the time approached to put in the afternoon line-up [midday], Bernhard and Per-Ulrik were something like 3 or 4 up with just five to play. Now, when I played in the Ryder Cup and won, I just couldn't wait to get out there and do it all again, so I put them together again. What a disaster.

'No sooner had I put my pairings in than it started to pour with rain and they [Langer and Johansson] started losing holes; more than an hour later they scraped home on the last green, but were soaked through, cold, and only had half an hour for a sandwich and a change of clothes. They were no match for a fresh, dry and fit Pavin and Mickelson. When I went into the team room that evening I told the team that if we lose the Ryder Cup by a point, they can blame me. It was my mistake; I got that one completely wrong.'

To be fair that was a reasonable and wholly understandable mistake to make – a decision based on sound reasoning and unlucky not to work out.

The only good news on that sodden afternoon came from the most unlikely of quarters: 'With Seve in such dreadful form, I had to give him a game before the singles, and frankly, better to get it out of the way on the first day rather than later. Obviously I couldn't put him in the foursomes as he would destroy both of them, so once again David Gilford comes into the picture.' Bearing in mind the poor hand he dealt Gilford at Kiawah Island, giving him Seve at Oak Hill looked an act of downright sadism! 'Remember, David is a very straight hitter, so he could get the pars and maybe Seve might come in with a birdie or two', was Gallacher's thought behind this unlikely pairing. 'Anyway, Seve inspired David. David played way above himself, he would say so himself, and Seve did what Seve does best, annoying the opposition, getting in the way, getting even an American crowd on their side, and they won handsomely.' They did have one of the US's weaker pairs in Brad Faxon and Peter Jacobsen, but Seve had got his point. An attempt to try to work the same miracle the following afternoon got the come-uppance it probably deserved.

The good news for Gilford? It got him another game the following morning with no less than Bernhard Langer, and that worked too. Three points for Europe that morning meant the sides were level going into the final fourballs, but Gallacher's attempt to get Faldo and Montgomerie to generate a couple of points playing apart (Montgomerie with Sam Torrance and Faldo with Langer) when they had only got 1 point from three games together came unstuck.

But in the case of Faldo and Langer, only just. Out last and with the other three matches going clearly one way or the other – two to the US and one to Europe – Faldo and Langer both played really well, but couldn't get ahead. They were matching one another par for par, with only the occasional birdie. Corey Pavin and Loren Roberts were only just hanging on, dovetailing just to keep in touch. It was a match that looked like going Europe's way, a half was the worst that could possibly happen.

All square playing the last, Europe even seemed to have the best of it as they came to the green, both our players some 15 or 18 feet away in two, with Roberts 20 yards away – on those greens no easy two-putt – and Pavin closest, but off the green at the back. 'I hoped that Roberts would struggle to get it close, and so leave Pavin with a most difficult shot to get dead, a chip all downhill and with a big swing,' said Gallacher still recalling every moment, even after all this time. 'But Roberts was always one of the very best putters and he laid it absolutely dead. As seemed to have been the case all afternoon, our two both just missed and then, with nothing to lose and the pin out, Pavin chipped in; just about the only way he could have even got it close.'

It had been a heroic struggle by Europe, but the points were divided that second day, and for the first time since 1981, America had the lead going into the singles. They had only once lost the singles in the Ryder Cup and that was at The Belfry in 1985, never in America. Surely, Bernard Gallacher's valiant third attempt was going to end up like the other two, in a narrow but irritating defeat.

With the American cheers still ringing in his ears from Pavin's chip in, Gallacher, perhaps for the first time roused from his normal phlegmatic self, declared passionately: 'the Americans can have their cheers on Saturday, we're going to have ours on Sunday!' In looking forward to the singles, just about the only hope was that the Americans might have paid too much attention to those cheers and feel the job was already done. 'In my first two Ryder Cups, I concentrated very much on where I wanted my players to play in the singles; I really didn't try and outguess the opposition, think where they might play this man or that,' was Gallacher's assessment of his early singles philosophy. 'I really liked to have a balanced spread, some power at the start, experience near the end as well as a bit here and there in the middle. I didn't want to put a batch of first time players out all together anywhere in the draw. This time I didn't have as many rookies and really tried to work out what Lanny would do and react accordingly.

'Being two ahead, and being the hard competitor that he is, I thought Wadkins would try and go out and win this thing quickly, have some good players out early, and keep a couple back to the end if things got tight. And that's what he did. I decided to put what I felt at the time to be my best and most experienced players in the middle. My biggest problem was what to do with Seve. Despite his short game, there was no way he could win a point and in the end I decided to put him out first. There was a fair chance he would get one of their good players, and that year Tom Lehman was very much one of the best, and if Seve was to go down, then let him take a big name with him.

'Seve was not best pleased with the idea at the time, but he preferred it to the other berth I suggested, going last. The thought that it might all come down to him, with the way his game was really didn't appeal! He knew in his heart I had to get rid of his point early on, so first it was and what a fantastic job he did. He was still all square after 10 holes, and what a fillip to the team that was, as they set off; it really gave them a boost to think he could keep such a player as Lehman tied up for that long.'

What Seve also did was take the limelight for the first couple of hours, enabling those immediately behind to get into their matches without too much in the way of television cameras and crowds to break their concentration. This was particularly helpful to Mark James and Howard Clark, who hadn't been out competitively since the Friday morning. Both got off to a good start and Clark – with the help of a hole-in-one at the 11th – held on to become the first of five European players to go to the final hole, four winning and Ian Woosnam getting another half with Fred Couples. Sometime before that James had put the first point on the board for Europe.

With Lehman finally getting the better of Seve, and Davis Love putting another early point on the board for the US, it was clear everything that could possibly go right had to, if this most improbable of wins was to happen. Monty soon put paid to Ben Crenshaw and Torrance took care of Roberts; then came the first of the critical moments.

Gilford was 1 up playing the last against Brad Faxon and, as you might expect, found the fairway off the tee. Faxon didn't, and with no option but to lay up a 100 yards short, it looked a relatively simple task for Gilford to put another point on the board for Europe. Now, while he is straight, Gilford is not long and he still had over 200 yards to go with his second. A long iron is not a club you want to be tackling the 18th at Oak Hill with, especially with the greens firm and this one perched up on the hill. He hit a fine shot, but it skipped just through the green and into some long grass.

Now, Gilford cannot chip, or certainly could not then. He was a mere 15 feet from the putting surface, with the pin just another 10 feet on the green and all downhill, the surface glassy. In some ways it was a shot not dissimilar to the one Pavin had holed the night before against Faldo and Langer, but Gilford's lie was far worse. By now it was apparent that a five might well be good enough, Faxon having played a good but not great third to some 15 feet.

Seve, and possibly only Seve, might have managed to flick the ball up from Gilford's lie and somehow get it to stop somewhere close on that slippery green. It was certainly beyond Gilford's capabilities. He took out a 7-iron, his aim somehow to dribble the ball through the rough and trickle onto the green. Try a normal shot, and there was a better than even chance he would not keep it on the green at all.

Seve, watching from behind the green could not believe it. 'Bernard,' he says to Gallacher, 'go and tell him he cannot run that through the rough; he must chip it.' Seve was already rehearsing the role of interfering captain he was to pursue in Spain two years later! Gallacher, of course, did no such thing. Gilford's destiny was literally in his own hands. Failing to get to the green was the lesser of two evils: too strong and he was bound to be miles away. He duly scuffed it, but got through most of the rough and, to his credit, he just about got the next one within 10 feet. Faxon, the great putter, missed and Gilford, again with all the fortunes of the Ryder Cup on his shoulders somehow managed to hole it. One of the vital musts from Europe's standpoint had happened, but there were still to be a couple more.

Nick Faldo was next. His form had not been great all week, but he was against Curtis Strange, who was also way below his best. Indeed, neither player seemed capable of raising his game sufficiently to win the match. Oak Hill finishes with three tough par-4s, and Strange could do no better than five at either of the first two, enabling Faldo to board the 18th tee all square. Both drove into trouble and could only play out short. Later there were those who credited Faldo with deliberately putting his shot into the semi rough, a swathe no more than 2 yards wide, so that his wedge to the green would not carry too much backspin, the pin being right up the back. When asked later, Faldo would only smile. Nevertheless, he hit by far the better approach, perhaps to 5 feet, and when Strange failed to get his four, Faldo kept his nerve, as you almost knew he would.

That left Philip Walton, whose game had fallen away during the week of the match. He did have one outing, a foursome, with Ian Woosnam on the second morning but lost that, so his confidence was not high. He was in the penultimate match and with Johansson by now down to Phil Mickelson immediately behind, Walton came to the 17th, 2 up and two to play against Jay Haas, the whole match his to win or lose. With the Americans holding the trophy only a win would bring it back to Europe. Walton had a putt for the match from 5 feet at 17, but missed. Haas was never going to make four at 18, but from the fairway Walton came up short, into deep grass on the bank in front of the green; far better than being long and up where David Gilford had been. For an agonising moment or two it seemed he might have lost his ball. He hadn't, but the lie was poor and he chipped modestly, still some 15 feet short. Somehow, with everything shaking, he got it close enough to be conceded.

There was no shame in Walton having the shakes – grown men were crying, and even in this astonishing series of contests over the 25 years from the early 1980s, this surely was the most amazing of them all. It almost passed unnoticed that, for the first time, America had lost the singles on their own soil. Perhaps they had been a bit too relaxed once they had a lead going into the final day.

Walton was the hero of the hour – the man who had

won the Ryder Cup, and the reception he got when he returned to his native Ireland lasted month after month. Maybe the whole experience was all too much. He would hardly ever compete again, within a year or two had lost his playing rights on the European Tour, and would only thereafter be seen in an occasional cameo role in some tournament he had previously won.

But 1995 was crucial in more ways than one. The great men who'd carried the burden of expectancy these past ten years, the major champions from the 1980s, were no longer the predominant point-gatherers of previous years. It was others who had mostly done the work this time. At the beginning of the week, Colin Montgomerie had echoed many peoples' thoughts when he said: 'If we don't win one of these again soon, we may never win one for years.' In 1995 the golfers of Europe proved to themselves the Ryder Cup could be won without the likes of Seve, Faldo, Langer, Woosnam, Lyle and Olazábal all playing at their very best.

For Bernard Gallacher it was just reward for six hard years, made harder by having to follow in the giant footsteps of Tony Jacklin. Perhaps it was the balance in his life – of having his job at Wentworth to go back to – that kept him sane particularly in the aftermath of those two disappointments in 1991 and 1993. 'As soon as the matches were over I was back in the shop at Wentworth. Win or lose the members would come in and wanted to chat about it; many of them had been to all the matches. They always brought me back to earth. There was the shop to run, games to play with the members and people to teach. It was they who kept things normal.

'When all is said and done, it was just a relief to win. They were all tough matches, close matches. Being captain doesn't really change your life. Sure, there are many more demands on your time; people want you to attend things, dinners and so forth. I didn't want to do that at first, I wanted to let it all sink in, but for a long time afterwards they still want to hear all the stories, and you repeat them, time and again. But that's nice, it keeps it all alive, fresh.'

CHAPTER SEVEN

Losing Not an Option in Spain

1997
Severiano Ballesteros

Close to twenty years after the Continentals first joined Great Britain and Ireland to try to wrest the Ryder Cup from the United States, 1997 was time for the match to be played in mainland Europe. Jack Nicklaus' suggestion back in the 1970s for it to be Europe rather than just Great Britain and Ireland had been more successful than he might have anticipated – or even wanted – but the addition of Continental players to 'our' team had played a significant part in making the event competitive.

There was never really any argument as to which country in Europe the match would go first. Apart from the players it had supplied throughout the 1980s and 1990s, Spain had been hugely supportive of the European Tour in its fledgling years. In the early spring or late autumn, when golf was no longer possible in

Valderrama

26–28 September

Europe (*Seve Ballesteros*)	Matches		USA (*Tom Kite*)
Fourballs: *Morning*			
J.M. Olazábal & C. Rocca (1 hole)	1	0	D. Love III & P. Mickelson
N. Faldo & L. Westwood	0	1	F. Couples & B. Faxon (1 hole)
J. Parnevik & P.-U. Johansson (1 hole)	1	0	T. Lehman & J. Furyk
B. Langer & C. Montgomerie	0	1	T. Woods & M. O'Meara (3/2)
Foursomes: *Afternoon*			
J.M. Olazábal & C. Rocca	0	1	S. Hoch & L. Janzen (1 hole)
B. Langer & C. Montgomerie (5/3)	1	0	T. Woods & M. O'Meara
N. Faldo & L. Westwood (3/2)	1	0	J. Leonard & J. Maggert
I. Garrido & J. Parnevik (halved)	½	½	P. Mickelson & T. Lehman (halved)
Fourballs: *Morning*			
C. Montgomerie & D. Clarke (1 hole)	1	0	F. Couples & D. Love III
I. Woosnam & T. Björn (2/1)	1	0	J. Leonard & B. Faxon
N. Faldo & L. Westwood (2/1)	1	0	T. Woods & M. O'Meara
J.M. Olazábal & I. Garrido (halved)	½	½	P. Mickelson & T. Lehman (halved)
Foursomes: *Afternoon*			
C. Montgomerie & B. Langer (1 hole)	1	0	L. Janzen & J. Furyk
N. Faldo & L. Westwood	0	1	S. Hoch & J. Maggert (2/1)
J. Parnevik & I. Garrido (halved)	½	½	T. Woods & J. Leonard (halved)
J.M. Olazábal & C. Rocca (5/4)	1	0	F. Couples & D. Love III
Singles			
I. Woosnam	0	1	F. Couples (8/7)
P.-U. Johansson (3/2)	1	0	D. Love III
C. Rocca (4/2)	1	0	T. Woods
T. Björn (halved)	½	½	J. Leonard (halved)
D. Clarke	0	1	P. Mickelson (2/1)
J. Parnevik	0	1	M. O'Meara (5/4)
J.M. Olazábal	0	1	L. Janzen (1 hole)
B. Langer (2/1)	1	0	B. Faxon
L. Westwood	0	1	J. Maggert (3/2)
C. Montgomerie (halved)	½	½	S. Hoch (halved)
N. Faldo	0	1	J. Furyk (3/2)
I. Garrido	0	1	T. Lehman (7/6)
Europe	14½	13½	**USA**

more northern parts, Spain would put together as many as half a dozen tournaments a year. They wouldn't be the biggest or the best, but they were competitive weeks at a time when the Tour was trying to provide a reasonable alternative to the overpowering might of the US Tour; and it was in the years before Europe began linking up with South Africa, Australia and the Far East to turn itself into a year-round circuit.

But it was the players that made Spain the natural choice. Seve Ballesteros led the way, and after Antonio Garrido joined him that first year in 1979, along came Manuel Pinero, José Maria Canizares, José Rivero and then the best of all Seve's acolytes, and his great partner for so many years, José Maria Olazábal. For a time the Continentals didn't make much of an impact, Seve and Garrido winning only 1 point out of 6 between them in 1979, and then Seve falling out with everybody in 1981 and not even playing. It wasn't till Tony Jacklin took him aside in 1982, drilled into him our awful track record in the match, showed him the possibilities if we could only become competitive, that Seve became imbued with a similar passion.

There was never any doubt that Seve would be captain when the match came to Spain. His ability to compete at the highest level had been on the wane for some years, and to do well in the Ryder Cup you have to be right at the top of your game. He had not been at his best four years previously at The Belfry, had asked to be left out of one of the series for the first time ever, and then been quite dreadful on the narrow, tree-lined fairways at Oak Hill two years after that. That said, he'd made his contribution by coaxing David Gilford to an unlikely fourball win, and then held the spotlight for a couple of hours against Tom Lehman in the singles, but the standard of his own play must have reduced him to tears. By 1997, there was never any question that he might still play.

So the country and the captain were sorted, it only remained for the right location to be chosen – not as straightforward as you might imagine. Every resort in Spain would have loved the Ryder Cup – the kudos, the exposure and the association would have lasted for years. Many hats were tossed into the ring, but the sheer logistics of staging this massive event were beyond the reach of all but a few. Had there been a course with the space and accessibility close to Madrid that probably would have been first choice; Madrid had always done its stuff on the tournament front, with a couple of events a year in Spain's heyday. But Madrid is a compact city with narrow streets, heavy traffic and would never have been able to deal with the sheer volume of people involved in the Ryder Cup.

Once Madrid was eliminated, one venue stood out above all others: Valderrama. Almost every year from the late 1980s it had hosted the season-ending Volvo Masters, apart from a few years, when one of the World Golf Championships came there instead. It had, therefore, a continuous tournament record, and although not long, its narrow fairways, small greens and exposure to the varied winds of southern Spain always made it tricky and testing.

The selection process had to be seen to be fair and democratic, even though some of the tactics employed by the candidates weren't. Jaime Ortiz-Patino – owner of Valderrama and a man with the resources to make the Ryder Cup work regardless of obstacles thrown up – looked to seal the deal early by signing Seve to his cause. In a convoluted arrangement he offered Seve a

share of future green fees, based on extra business gen-
erated by the Ryder Cup, which would earn Seve close
to $1 million. For some months Seve's business team
haggled around the details and then at the last minute
Seve threw his weight behind another of the candidates, Novo Sancti Petri, a course Seve had designed
near Cadiz.

All this was complicated by the fact Seve was sitting
on the Ryder Cup committee, which had the final say in
where the match was played! As it transpired, Nuovo
Santi Petri was unsuitable for half a dozen reasons and
despite some respectable bids from the likes of El Saler
in Valencia, and Monte Castillo near Jerez – both of
which could have handled the event – Valderrama and
Jaime Ortiz-Patino duly got the nod. It was to be a great
decision in view of the many logistical hurdles that
would be thrown up before the match and the vile
weather during it.

Seve would have one other serious matter to deal
with before the match got underway, and it concerned
one of his fellow countrymen, Miguel Martin. Mainly
as a result of winning the Heineken Classic in Australia
at the start of the year, Martin had played his way onto
the team, albeit in last place. With the best will in the
world Martin was little more than a journeyman and
Valderrama almost certain to be his only Ryder Cup:
understandably, he was very keen to play. Some weeks
before the match he damaged his wrist and was out
for the best part of two months, but insisted that it
would be sufficiently healed for him to play at
Valderrama.

You might make allowances for a tried-and-tested star
to get better, as Bernard Gallacher had done with José
Maria Olazábal back in 1995, but a first-timer coming to

the Ryder Cup not having played for some time was not what you wanted. Also, waiting in the wings in 11th place in the points list, was none other than Olazábal himself, just back from that debilitating illness and with not quite enough time to qualify as of right.

Seve decided that Miguel Martin must not play and for a couple of weeks a rather unseemly public brawl played out, as he tried to persuade Martin to do the honourable thing and stand down. To the casual observer – and the passionate supporter of the European cause – the removal of Martin and the insertion in his place of Olazábal was absolutely to be desired. Thank goodness all the participants were Spanish – can you imagine a captain of some other nationality attempting to play Seve's hand and getting away with it! As in all things that really mattered to him, Seve got his way: Martin got in the official team photo, was awarded his colours so to speak, and Seve got Ollie in the team without having to expend one of his wildcards.

After six years and three matches under the captaincy of Bernard Gallacher, playing for Seve was a totally different experience: 'Seve was always the leader, just couldn't help himself,' recalls Colin Montgomerie. 'Here we were in Spain; losing just wasn't an option. It was Seve and the King of Spain; you felt you were part of an irresistible force.'

The Ryder Cup at Valderrama will always be remembered for Seve dashing about in his captain's buggy, seemingly everywhere at once and, to those steeped in the traditions of the game, taking the prerogative of the captain being able to give advice to his players during a match way beyond acceptable practice: 'You have to remember, Seve was still only 40, and really felt he should still be playing', Montgomerie sensed. 'All what appeared to be his interfering came from that. Of course he brought incredible passion to the job and you were very much swept up in the whole emotion of the thing. Once you were committed to the cause though, he really was a bit of a nuisance.'

Seve saw it differently: 'With important matches, or matches that were close near the end, I tried to get to the tee before they drove. I knew the Americans were always aware of my presence and I think it made them uncomfortable. It always seemed to me we won the hole when I was there.' Surely only Seve could look you in the eye and make that remark without any sense of irony! 'I also knew the course better than anyone,' he went on, 'so there were many occasions I could help with what shot to play. I won many matchplay titles and sometimes you have to try different things than you would in medal. Jesper Parnevik and Per-Ulrik Johansson were playing the 4th, and even before Tom Lehman played, Per-Ulrik had an 8-iron out to lay up. I say "wait until you see what he does before you decide." When Lehman hit it on the green, Per-Ulrik then took a 3-wood and also put it on the green.'

Seve's captaincy was not the democratic rule of Gallacher, it was much nearer a dictatorship. In one of the practice rounds the seasoned quartet of Faldo, Woosnam, Langer and Montgomerie were on the 17th green, a hole that Seve had recently redesigned. Up comes Seve and his buggy, leaps out and questions the group on how they had played the hole; had they laid up, had they gone for the green in two, where had they driven to, that sort of thing. He did not like the answers, and had this illustrious quartet buggied back to the tee to play it all over again, the way he felt it should be played!

Nor was Seve steeped in the finer tenets of man man-agement. In the days leading up to the match, he only really spoke to a handful of the more experienced and successful players – the likes of Langer, Montgomerie and Olazábal: the rest he largely ignored. Ian Woosnam he suspected of not being fully fit, having been at Ian Botham's son's wedding the weekend before, and so didn't play him till the second day and only once before the singles. That Woosnam would take one of the new boys, Thomas Björn, and with him beat Justin Leonard and Brad Faxon wouldn't have changed Seve's opinion one iota.

It was a tough baptism for those playing their first Ryder Cup, the tremendous razzmatazz of this first playing of the match outside the UK, and a captain not wholly sympathetic to the insecurities of those for whom it was a whole new experience. Nevertheless, three of them – Björn, Darren Clarke and Lee Westwood – would go on to become very much part of European successes for the next decade. Björn in particular was somewhat scathing of his captain. When talking about his singles match against Justin Leonard, in which he lost the first four holes, then rallied to be 1 up and one to play, only to lose the last to halve, he said: 'Seve walked with me those first four holes, then fortunately went somewhere else.' What happened at the last? 'Seve reappeared!'

Darren Clarke was nervous too, and made more so by being largely ignored by his captain. He too wouldn't play till the second day, but at least was given the best possible berth, having Monty as his partner. All square and two to play in the morning fourball against the for-midable pairing of Fred Couples and Davis Love,

Darren in the rough at 17 and Monty on the fairway, when along comes Seve again: 'Darren's ball was lying quite well,' recalls Monty, 'but the obvious play was for him to lay up and then I could go for the green; I was well within range. But no, Seve insisted Darren have a go for it, which he did, and well as he hit it, didn't make the carry. I now had to lay up; the risk of both of us going in the pond was too great. I hit it to 58 yards, the fairways still sopping wet, and there's Seve at my side telling me, "hit it in softly, feel it in". In the end I had to tell him to p*** off. Fortunately I did hit a good shot and holed the putt to go 1 up, and a half at the last was good enough.'

For all his mistakes in the subtle art of man management, and his cavalier attitude to the privileges of being captain, Seve brought phenomenal passion to the job, and that compensated for most of his indiscretions. He was, after all, Seve, and he played the role of captaincy much as he had played the game of golf – often naughty, outrageous, but his infectious *joi de vivre* enabled him to tread on toes, stretch the boundaries of what's acceptable, and get away with it. And of course, he won. For him, that was everything, as it was for most of us.

Some things he did well. His pairings showed a deep understanding of matching like with like, putting old hands with young talent. Nick Faldo was put in charge of Lee Westwood and together they gathered 2 points out of 4, including a victory over Tiger Woods and Mark O'Meara. Woosnam and Björn got a point, even though both had played only once before the Sunday. Olazábal and Costantino Rocca won 2 points out of 3, and his banker pairing of Monty and Langer also won twice from three outings. Langer, by now a veteran, was given the second morning off to be fit and ready for the singles.

Seve thought long and hard about all aspects of his task. Never one to be hidebound by tradition, he decided that foursomes first were not in the best interests of his team, particularly with four rookies in it. For the first time ever, it was to be fourballs in the morning, foursomes in the afternoon, and so get everyone hitting their own ball as soon as possible. This sort of change is very much in the gift of the home captain, and while Ben Crenshaw, a great traditionalist, would change back two years later, Sam Torrance reversed it once again at The Belfry in 2002, and that is the way it has stayed ever since. Paul Azinger though, went back to foursomes first for the 2008 match at Valhalla.

The 1997 American team was different to that at Oak Hill, and considerably stronger. Gone were Peter Jacobsen, Ben Crenshaw, Curtis Strange, Loren Roberts and Corey Pavin. The Pavin of 1995 would have been a great asset, but shortly after his US Open win of 1995 he had been seduced by a lucrative club contract, gave up his old, quirky Cleveland irons and was never the same again. Into the side came Justin Leonard, by now a major champion after winning The Open at Troon that summer; Mark O'Meara, who would win two of the following year's majors; Lee Janzen, a year short of winning the US Open for the second time; a young Jim Furyk; and of course the recently arrived Tiger Woods. All in all an up-and-coming side with much dead wood removed and, man for man, more powerful than their opponents.

To balance this, the match was at Valderrama. Originally laid out by Robert Trent Jones, it is surprisingly and pleasantly old-fashioned in design. The greens are small, the fairways narrow, and it is a course that takes a lot of getting to know. There is relatively little rough, but the cork trees lining most fairways give great definition and are far more damaging to errant tee shots than the long rough and shallow fairway bunkers of the modern American course. Perched high up in the hills overlooking Soto Grande, it is also exposed to variable winds either from the North African coast or from the hinterland: rare is the day when neither blows at some point.

Most importantly, top European players had been playing there competitively for the best part of ten years. Three days were by no means sufficient to unlock all its secrets, and three days were all the Americans had. Seve certainly didn't miss the opportunity to tweak the course to suit his team's chances: 'They were longer off the tee than we were, so with the help of John Paramour, the tournament referee, instead of the fairways widening out the further you hit it, I had it narrowed down past 300 yards. At the 11th, Tiger Woods, Fred Couples and Davis Love could never use their driver.' This practice of tuning a course to give the home team an advantage had been pioneered by Jacklin during his time, and has been part of European preparations for the match, when at home, ever since.

After an opening ceremony – Spanish horses, flamenco dancers and the King of Spain – that transcended anything either Britain or the United States had ever put on (sadly, as both the US and Europe tried thereafter to outdo each other in the splendour of the pageant, and quality was ever after sacrificed for quantity) the opening day was dreadful. Overnight the heavens opened and the southern half of Spain was drenched for the best part of twelve hours. As players, officials and spectators stood about in the pre-dawn gloom watching the rain pour down, the odds against a shot being hit that day seemed enormous.

But an unforeseen benefit of being at Valderrama manifested itself. Jaime Ortiz-Patino had spared nothing in making his pride and joy the best course in mainland Europe. Securing the Ryder Cup had been his Holy Grail and he then left nothing to chance in making sure the event was an unmitigated triumph. As part of his preparations, he had put in a drainage system that could have emptied the Mediterranean if there had been somewhere to send it. The rains stopped sometime after 9.00 am and to everyone's amazement, play was possible around 11.30. The knock-on effect though, was that that day's play wasn't completed, nor was the second day finished on time.

For obvious reasons the first morning – whether you are captaining Europe or America – you put out your best players in the first series. Everyone wants to get off to a good start. A brief look at Europe's pairings and it certainly seemed this was one of the strongest line-ups we had ever been able to field. Continuing Seve's strong Latin theme, José Maria Olazábal and Costantino Rocca went first, and whatever else, Davis Love and Phil Mickelson would not have understood a word they were saying. Strangely perhaps, Love was not sent out immediately with his great friend Fred Couple, with whom he had had such a successful time in the World Cup, winning four years in a row in the early 1990s.

Once again though, the American pairings during the first two days showed their fixation with giving everyone a game each day. They have always seemed prepared to break up even successful partnerships to stick rigidly to this principle, regardless of form shown in the practice rounds. It is almost as though they don't wish to highlight anyone who may be playing poorly – that and the belief that if you have played your way onto the side then you have earned the right to play each day. A chivalrous way to play the hand when America was winning every contest by a handful of points, but now that Europe was more than competitive and was regularly building considerable leads going into the singles, maybe it was time for America to rethink this strategy.

Perhaps the only surprise in Seve's run up to the match had been the choice of Jesper Parnevik over Padraig Harrington. Harrington, though a pro for just two years, had already won the Spanish Open in 1996, and had been a member of Great Britain and Ireland's successful Walker Cup team of 1995. Those familiar with his game knew him to be a born match player, and as a great scrambler, most difficult to play against. Perhaps though, with four newcomers already in the team, Seve felt Parnevik's experience would be more valuable. As it turned out, he would contribute a win in the first series with Johansson, and 2 invaluable half-points in long drawn foursomes matches with Ignacio Garrido. Both these matches finished the morning after the afternoon on which they had started. By the singles, he and Garrido were spent, but had more than done their job.

With an 11.30 am start, and the first series being fourballs, most of that opening day was consumed by the first four games, especially as three out of the four went to the last green. Olazábal and Rocca did their captain proud, beating Love and Mickelson 1 up, and Parnevik and Johansson eventually did the same to Tom Lehman and Jim Furyk. They had been going comfortably, a couple up midway through the back nine, but at that moment Seve chose to inform them that Johansson would not be playing in the second series, despite being the main provider of birdies round the turn. This spoilt their rhythm, and they only just squeaked home. Most surprisingly, Faldo/Westwood and Langer/Montgomerie both lost, the latter to the much-anticipated pairing of Tiger Woods and Mark O'Meara.

Here Seve showed nerve and understanding, keeping both partnerships together for the afternoon four-somes and was rewarded with points from both. Monty and Langer reversed that morning's defeat against Woods and O'Meara, while Parnevik and Garrido finally shook hands for half a point that Saturday morning. Europe had their noses in front.

The second series of fourballs was where Europe eased away. Monty and Clarke, despite Seve's running interference, led the way against Couples and Love, this obvious pairing finally getting two outings that day, but with nothing to show for it at the end. Maybe US cap-tain Tom Kite was right at the start not to put them together! Faldo and Westwood were now into their stride and gave Woods and O'Meara their second defeat – starting Woods on his way to a Ryder Cup record of which he will never be proud.

Ian Woosnam and Thomas Björn got their 1 point on their only outing the first two days and the one time the Spanish pairing of Olazábal and Garrido got together, they managed half a point against Mickelson and Lehman. The highlight of this game was Garrido getting a full tutorial from Seve as to how to play downhill from the bunker behind the 17th green and duly getting it close enough for a half in four.

Another 2½ points came in the final series of four-somes, with Seve once again getting in on the act as Monty and Langer were trying to get the better of Lee Janzen and Jim Furyk. One up and one to play, Monty for once missed the 18th fairway on the right, under the trees: 'Seve was there waiting, even before Langer could get to the ball', recalls Monty, the memory still fresh a decade later. 'He had already seen some impossible escape route, a sort of high-flying 3-iron, between branches and a couple of changes of direction, that would get the ball to the green. Only Seve could have thought such a shot possible, and certainly only Seve might have brought it off! Even while he was trying to convince Bernhard that this was the shot to play, Bernhard chipped out onto the fairway.

'The Americans meanwhile found the front of the green. We were on in three, and not that close. With the light fading, and no one believing any of the matches would come down the 18th that day, they had already rolled and triple cut that green in preparation for the early start the following day. Unaware of this, and with the pin at the back, the Americans putted off the green; a 5 was good enough for a half and a win!'

The lead with the singles to come was the biggest Europe had ever taken into the final day, 10½–5½, 5 whole points. At that point, after days seemingly without sleep (various people vouch that he rang them during the week at odd times of the night to discuss progress), Seve finally relaxed. It seemed he of all people thought the job had been done. After days of deep intensity, of keeping his team constantly on their toes, frightened of losing and being made to feel they had failed their leader, he sat back and asked who wanted to play where!

Ignacio Garrido said he would like to go last. He still had his second day foursome to finish and would obviously like as long as possible to recover before going out again. But a rookie in last place? What if the day goes wrong and it all comes down to his match? Then Ian Woosnam, having played only one game out of the four and being light on competitive action that week, asked to go out first. He would have a responsibility to give the lead and get a positive score on the board early, and it would not be as stressful as going out later and finding that it could all come down to his game.

At this point some of the old guard sensed that all this sudden democracy was getting out of hand, and quietly teamed up, telling Seve what they thought was best. As a result, matches 8 to 11 involved Olazábal, Langer, Monty and Faldo, just to tidy things up should it get close. And it did!

Woosnam played the first two holes poorly and was promptly swamped by Fred Couples. Couples, by then having spent nearly twenty years on tour, was still a majestic player capable of superb golf, but could be fragile under pressure. The only way to play successfully against him was to stick with him in the knowledge that in a tight corner his short putting was suspect. He and Woosnam had played one another in the singles both at The Belfry in 1993 and at Oak Hill two years later and halved on each occasion. What had looked a good opening encounter became a beacon for the beleaguered American team. If it had been cricket, Europe had just lost an early wicket.

e man who started it all and who donated the handsome trophy – the seed merchant
m Verulam, Samuel Ryder.

Great Britain and Ireland won the first two matches played at home, here at Moortown
1929 and four years later at Southport and Ainsdale, but they would then have to w
another 24 years before winning again.

Sam Ryder presenting the trophy to George Duncan, the Great Britain and Ireland ca
tain, at Moortown in 1929.

1957 only Dai Rees and Ken Bousfield won a point in the foursomes, but a captain's nings from Rees in the singles brought Great Britain and Ireland their only victory in a -year spell from the 1930s to the 1980s.

ck Nicklaus, whose track record warranted two matches as captain, but who in the end came the first American captain to lose on home soil.

How appropriate, at almost the rebirth of the Ryder Cup in 1985, that the trophy shou have been presented to Tony Jacklin by Sam Ryder's granddaughter.

Seve and Jacklin at Muirfield Village, 1987. Together they rolled back 60 years of Ryc Cup history.

ny Jacklin with wife Astrid in 1989. The ladies of the Ryder Cup were an important part
Jacklin's strategy.

Seve at Kiawah Island in 1991. His driving wasn't that straight even then, but for Seve, he could hit it, he could hole it.

lesteros and Olazábal at Kiawah Island, 1991. The best Ryder Cup picture ever, and of
e best Ryder Cup partnership.

do and Montgomerie at Oak Hill, 1995. By then Monty was no. 1 in Europe, but in the
der Cup Faldo still called the shots.

Seve at Valderrama in Spain, 1997. Losing just wasn't an option.

...ods and O'Meara with captain Tom Kite at Valderrama, and Woods' introduction to the ...y different stresses and strains of team match play.

...r too many spectators were allowed into Brookline in 1999, a major contributing factor ... the distasteful way in which the match concluded.

Parnevik and Garcia at Brookline, 1999. The exuberance of youth and the start of Serg
Garcia's great Ryder Cup career.

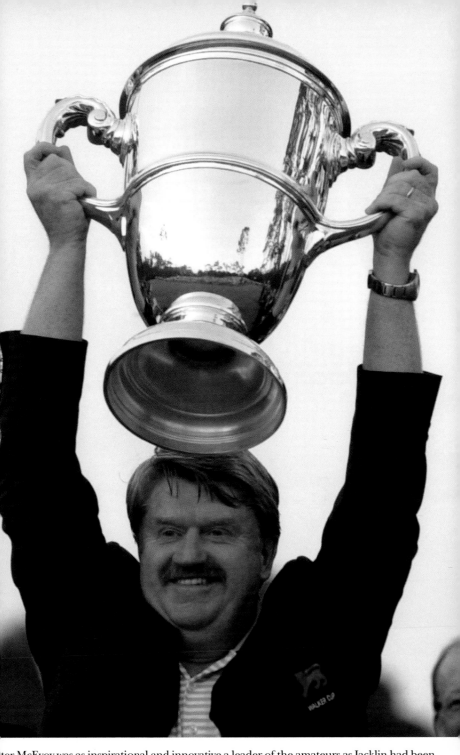

ter McEvoy was as inspirational and innovative a leader of the amateurs as Jacklin had been
 the professionals. His most satisfying moment was when the USGA set up a committee to
amine why it was they were suddenly losing more Walker Cups than they were winning.

To Paul McGinley fell the honour – and the joy – of holing the winning putt in 2002.

There was a year of waiting due to 9/11, but for Sam Torrance the wait was well worthwhile.

Woods and Mickelson, partners in fourballs and foursomes in 2004, were a misguided pairing that damaged America's effort right from the start, and brought much criticism on captain Hal Sutton.

Langer's captaincy was flawless, but the hat may just about have been the best part of Hal Sutton's efforts.

ke Donald, one of several newcomers to Europe's cause that have helped them to ntinue winning long after the clutch of Major champions from the 1980s had departed e scene.

06 was an emotional Ryder Cup for both Tiger Woods and Darren Clarke. Woods lost father in the spring and Clarke his wife Heather, to cancer, just weeks before the match.

Montgomerie at the K Club. The talisman of Europe's endeavour from 1991 to the present d

Per-Ulrik Johansson and Costantino Rocca soon righted the ship, Johansson beating Davis Love 3/2, completing a rotten week for Love, who played four games and lost the lot. Rocca did even better, beating Tiger Woods, also on the 16th green: that was 2 of the 4 points needed for victory. Then things got ugly.

Thomas Björn lost the first four holes to Justin Leonard (and only in the nick of time did Seve go elsewhere!), so that match looked gone; O'Meara was soon well up against Parnevik, who'd been involved in those two long-drawn-out affairs with Garrido, and was frankly spent before he went out. Mickelson was quickly 3 up on Darren Clarke, who in the end did well to take the match to the 16th, so once again things were getting tight.

But Olazábal was 2 up and three to play against Lee Janzen. Bernhard Langer, despite being brought back to all square from 3 up early on, then eased away and soon closed out Brad Faxon by 2/1. Monty was down most of the way to Scot Hoch, but pars at 14 and 16 were good enough to put him ahead for the first time, and he seemed to have momentum on his side. But that was it, Faldo played in lacklustre fashion to lose 3/2 to Jim Furyk, a player who had yet to show his full potential, and Garrido could only go through the motions, eventually losing to Tom Lehman by 7/6.

So it was close, but if we could get a point from Olazábal and Montgomerie, then all would be well. Suddenly, a ray of sunshine from an unexpected source. Tommy Björn had not only got back to all square against Leonard, but was actually 1 up and one to play: win that and Europe were home and dry.

But Björn lost the final hole (Seve had returned!), and then Olazábal lost the last three holes to Janzen, and with it a match the Europeans had assumed was theirs. Now the overall match was too close for comfort once again. Monty then lost the 17th. With the last two matches already gone, if he lost the 18th, Europe would have blown a 5-point lead.

Two weeks prior to the match, at the Lancome Trophy in Versailles, Monty had done an in-depth interview with Sky Sports, in which he charted his growing seniority in the Ryder Cup through the various slots in which he had played in the singles. In 1991 at Kiawah Island, as a rookie, he'd been hidden away in the middle, but did his reputation no harm by coming back from 4 down and four to play against Mark Calcavecchia to halve. Two years later, he was promoted to third in the team order and duly delivered an early point for Bernard Gallacher. At Oak Hill he was part of Gallacher's strong middle order, which produced that astonishing last-day fight back. Now he ruminated that he was ready for the ultimate test and said he hoped he would be somewhere down towards the end at Valderrama, somewhere like 10th spot, and that the whole contest might depend on the outcome of his match. He was indeed playing in the 10th match and had his wish! A half would do, but a win would be a win and so much nicer.

Hoch missed the fairway, and as is so often the case at Valderrama, could not go for the green in two. Monty split the fairway. Hoch made it to the green in three, but was 30 feet away; Monty was comfortably on in two and had two putts for an almost certain win. He got it stone-dead for at worst a half and so victory for Europe. Then Seve intervened for one last time. In the gathering gloom he instructed Monty to concede Hoch's putt, a putt which, under the circumstances,

Hoch would have been most unlikely to hole. The final result was by that narrowest of margins: 14½–13½. It had been much harder than it might have been, but Seve had delivered, in his own inimitable style, victory in Spain.

The Country Club

24–26 September

Europe (*Mark James*)	Matches		USA (*Ben Crenshaw*)
Foursomes: *Morning*			
C. Montgomerie & P. Lawrie (3/2)	1	0	D. Duval & P. Mickelson
J. Parnevik & S. Garcia (2/1)	1	0	T. Lehman & T. Woods
M.A. Jiménez & P. Harrington (halved)	½	½	D. Love III & P. Stewart (halved)
D. Clarke & L. Westwood	0	1	H. Sutton & J. Maggert (3/2)
Fourballs: *Afternoon*			
C. Montgomerie & P. Lawrie (halved)	½	½	D. Love III & J. Leonard (halved)
J. Parnevik & S. Garcia (1 hole)	1	0	P. Mickelson & J. Furyk
M.A. Jiménez & J.M. Olazábal (2/1)	1	0	H. Sutton & J. Maggert
D. Clarke & L. Westwood (1 hole)	1	0	D. Duval & T. Woods
Foursomes: *Morning*			
C. Montgomerie & P. Lawrie	0	1	H. Sutton & J. Maggert (1 hole)
D. Clarke & L. Westwood (3/2)	1	0	J. Furyk & M. O'Meara
M.A. Jiménez & P. Harrington	0	1	S. Pate & T. Woods (1 hole)
J. Parnevik & S. Garcia (3/2)	1	0	P. Stewart & J. Leonard
Fourballs: *Afternoon*			
D. Clarke & L. Westwood	0	1	P. Mickelson & T. Lehman (2/1)
J. Parnevik & S. Garcia (halved)	½	½	D. Love III & D. Duval (halved)
M.A. Jiménez & J.M. Olazábal (halved)	½	½	J. Leonard & H. Sutton (halved)
C. Montgomerie & P. Lawrie (2/1)	1	0	S. Pate & T. Woods
Singles			
L. Westwood	0	1	T. Lehman (3/2)
D. Clarke	0	1	H. Sutton (4/2)
J. Sandelin	0	1	P. Mickelson (4/3)
J. Van de Velde	0	1	D. Love III (6/5)
A. Coltart	0	1	T. Woods (3/2)
J. Parnevik	0	1	D. Duval (5/4)
P. Harrington (1 hole)	1	0	M. O'Meara
M.A. Jiménez	0	1	S. Pate (2/1)
J.M. Olazábal (halved)	½	½	J. Leonard (halved)
C. Montgomerie (1 hole)	1	0	P. Stewart
S. Garcia	0	1	J. Furyk (4/3)
P. Lawrie (4/3)	1	0	J. Maggert
Europe	13½	14½	**USA**

CHAPTER EIGHT

No Tea Party in Boston

1999
Mark James

The Country Club at Brookline, Massachusetts should have been a great venue for the 1999 Ryder Cup. It is one of America's grand old clubs, has hosted the US Open on three occasions and the Walker Cup twice. It is at its best in autumn, the trees just turning, late summer days beginning with a touch of mist and blossoming into glorious sunlit afternoons. It was also the heartland of where America best defends itself against marauding intruders.

Just half an hour from the centre of Boston and little more than a couple of miles from where the American War of Independence began, The Country Club is hardly changed from when it first opened its doors – not as a golf course but as a racecourse. The golf course hadn't long been laid out when the US Open first came here in 1913. It was the championship that changed the course of golfing history. That was when Francis Ouimet, a little-known American, took on the champions of the day from Great Britain, Harry Vardon and Ted Ray, tied them in normal play and beat them in a play-off. From that day on, America took the game's high ground and never really released it. The home side would have felt good about coming to The Country Club, as no American individual or team had ever lost there. Curtis Strange was the last to defend his nation's honour there, beating Nick Faldo in a play-off for the US Open in 1988.

Almost from the start, little things – side issues really – started to go wrong in the run up to the match. As well as being the most erudite of cities with institutions such as Harvard and the Massachusetts Institute of Technology, Boston is probably America's second most important financial centre after Wall Street. In 1999 America was at the height of the long bull run that saw out the end of the 20th century and huge quantities of money were being made in that tiny corner of New England. The demand for corporate hospitality was colossal, way in excess of what could ever have been supplied, however big the location.

The Country Club may have all the history and tradition you could want, but being old and private, unlimited space was just what it didn't have. Even so, the PGA of America managed to squeeze in $30 million worth of corporate marquees – and that was without a cork being popped or a canapé swallowed. That didn't leave an awful lot of space for the paying public to move around, and as with the marquees, the demand for tickets way exceeded supply.

Just as these numbers began to be bandied about – and it wasn't long before the total revenue figure was heard to be an astounding $65 million – the American players realised the PGA of America (the body representing the club pros over there, but still responsible for staging the Ryder Cup) were making a mint out of this. The players were putting in the blood, sweat and tears – that's why it had become so competitive – but they had nothing in the bank to show for it. No one was about to feel sorry for the state of the players' finances though, and in the end it was agreed that $100,000 would be donated to a charity of each player's choosing, and that's the way it has remained since 1999.

By now, Mark James had taken over the European captaincy. With Tony Jacklin having had the job for the best part of a decade, and then Bernard Gallacher leading the team for three matches immediately after, there had been some thought of Seve Ballesteros at least having a chance to reprise his success at Valderrama: historically, Ryder Cup captains had often had two goes, one at home and one away. Seve wisely realised he would probably never get away with his cavalier style of captaincy a second time – with his own players, let alone the opposition – and declined. He also wanted to focus on his own game.

James has already written his own book describing what happened in Boston nearly ten years ago, so the intricate details of that difficult week can be read in his memoir entitled *Into the Bear Pit*. Obviously, on several fronts, it was a trying time, and not just during the week of the match itself. The first test of his decision making came at the time of finalising the team three weeks before.

For much of the summer of 1991 there had been a distinct possibility James might play his way onto his own team. Indeed, he might well have done so right up to and including the final event, the BMW International in Munich. All summer long the media were dying to know if he would play if he qualified; and assuming a 'yes', then what would happen to the captaincy?

'No cards have ever been played closer to a chest,' James writes in his book. 'At the time of my appointment, my agreement with the Tour, and Ken Schofield in particular, was I would of course play. I just didn't make it clear at the outset, because I did not think that was the way it should be done. Sam Torrance [along with James the most obvious candidate to follow Seve, but still with ambitions to play] was himself trying to make the side and right from the start it was agreed I would hand the captaincy over to the other of my eventual assistants, Ken Brown. I knew the moment I said "Yes, I'll play if I qualify," the press would then want to know who would replace me. Although he'd agreed to act as stand in, Ken did not want all the fuss and bother that went with the territory.'

In the event James didn't make his own side, so attention immediately focused on who would be his two wild-card selections: 'Originally it had looked to be an easy decision with Jesper Parnevik and Sergio Garcia getting the nod. Garcia had only turned pro that year and had already won the Irish Open, but didn't look to have enough time to qualify as of right. Then in August he finished runner-up to Tiger Woods in the US PGA and played himself right into the team.'

Suddenly there were a host of candidates for the second birth. It was already apparent this was going to be a new-look team compared with previous years: Paul Lawrie and Jan Van de Velde – with their amazing one and two in The Open Championship – had played their way in; then Jarmo Sandelin and Miguel Angel Jiménez had both won twice in Europe; so along with Garcia and Padraig Harrington, six newcomers would be included in the team. That was already more than Europe had ever had going into this draining competition since Tony Jacklin had made it such an absorbing contest.

For the first time ever since the 1980s, none of those great major winners – Seve, Langer, Faldo and Woosnam – made the team as of right, and if any were to be there it would be courtesy of the captain, James. Both Faldo and Langer were at the BMW and of the two, on that year's form, Langer was the more likely choice, but even he had had a pretty modest summer. Then there were numbers 11 and 12 on the order of merit, Robert Karlsson and Andrew Coltart. It was to be one of those three, Parnevick already being assured of his place through fine play in the United States.

By the time the last putt had been holed in the BMW International in Germany and the press conference for the team announcement set up, informed opinion had it that, in view of the number of first-timers already in the side, Bernhard Langer would get the nod – a view enhanced when James was caught on camera talking to him between a couple of marquees near the press tent. However, he was only breaking the bad news. James has always been very much his own man and has, for much of his career, kept people offside by doing and saying the unexpected. This was another such occasion. He went for the outsider of the three, Andrew Coltart, to be his second choice along with Jesper Parnevik. Pick either of the other two, Robert Karlsson in 11th place or Langer, and no one would have thought other than he had made a reasoned choice in a most difficult situation. Many would have questioned the wisdom of adding another rookie, when the team already contained so many: 'Having decided to go with an in form newcomer rather than a somewhat out of form older but more experienced player,' James wrote in his book, 'I chose Andrew as he had had the better form over the last couple of months, had been the more consistent of the two.' It was as simple as that, and as ever with these sorts of decisions, had Europe come away with a victory at Brookline, with Coltart picking up a point or two, James would have been a hero. But that wasn't the way it worked out.

It had been a trying few weeks, what with his own serious attempt to make the team and then the stress of choosing the last couple of players. Ask any captain and he will tell you one of the most difficult parts of the job is having to explain to aspiring players your reasons for not including them. Within a day or two of getting back from Germany James had developed shingles and was convinced stress had been a big contributing factor.

In the build-up to the match James didn't put a foot wrong. Sam Torrance and Ken Brown were his vice-captains. It was a good team and as James and Torrance were still regulars on tour, and Brown was there a lot of the time as a commentator, all knew the players really well. With six Continentals in the side it might have been nice to have one of their own in the management structure, but that would have been nit-picking: everyone spoke good English.

The basic tenets of good Ryder Cup captaincy, as laid down during the Jacklin years, were now firmly established: everything that could be done to build team spirit was done. Between team selection and the match, the Lancome Trophy was played at Versailles and James used the occasion to host a dinner at the Trianon

Palace, inviting Ballesteros to attend: 'Get Seve on the subject of the Ryder Cup and you can listen to him all night, because he's been there and done everything, been part of all those incidents and experiences', James wrote in his book.

By now, anyone who took on the Ryder Cup captaincy knew it could not be done on a part-time basis. All captains were now current or ex-Tour players and brought the same intensity, single-mindedness and attention to detail to the task as they had to their own golf careers. They had to allow the captaincy to take over their lives totally, in order to do the job properly. They had to acquire man management, time allocation and communication skills, many of which they had little need of until taking on the responsibility of captaincy.

Being Mark James, he had had the odd run-in with the press over the years. The week of the Ryder Cup he realised, particularly being in America, how important the media, and particularly the journalists could be to the cause and went out of his way to work with them, meeting as many of their often repetitive demands as he could. When on form he can give them good copy indeed; that week he certainly did. While his own people could follow the dry, wry, often ironical responses he often came up with, the subtlety was usually lost on the American press: 'At one stage they wanted to know about how hostile the rivalry could become,' writes James in his book. 'I replied not too much as we all had mutual friends on the other side. I then finished by saying, "it's serious because we're both out here to win, but at the end of the week I'll be able to shake Ben warmly by the throat and we'll sit down and have a beer together." James, of course, gets maximum value from his lines, delivering them, as he does, in a Yorkshire accent and with not a flicker of change in his expression.

Three full days of practice before any competition is probably a couple too many for modern professionals. If they have never played a course before then they might try to play it twice in practice: one, perhaps, being in the Wednesday pro-am. With all their long shots played from yardage charts and with a full repertoire of recovery shots at their disposal, they need little in the way of local knowledge to be able to play a course competently from the start.

The Ryder Cup is different. There are partnerships to create or confirm, there's a bit of matchplay mentality to acquire, and in America they often go to some of these classic old courses that are quite quirky. They are US Open venues mostly, and take a fair amount of understanding. The Country Club was right in that league. You also have to fit in – and recover from – the welcome dinner, the gala evening, and The Opening ceremony: so the three days of build-up soon flash by.

With over half the team never having played in the Ryder Cup before, every pairing was going to be new. Some looked obvious on paper and all worked well in practice. The two Scots, Montgomerie and Lawrie, had similar games – neat and tidy – and both liked to play quickly. It also met the usual prerequisite of putting an old hand with a first timer. It was easy to see them playing together and playing top. Lee Westwood and Darren Clarke were by now very good chums, both with a Ryder Cup behind them, but with the chance of forging a new partnership that could last some time.

Sergio Garcia was playing a lot in America and knew Jesper Parnevik well: here again the perfect opportunity to put an experienced player with one of the new boys. Lastly, it seemed obvious to play the two remaining Spaniards, José Maria Olazábal and Miguel Angel Jiménez (good friends of long standing) together and even though Jiménez was the elder, it was his first match, so once again, old with young.

The only problem was that Olazábal was suffering from his perennial problem, erratic driving – destructive in foursomes but containable in fourballs. Fortunately, of the remaining four, all first-time players, Padraig Harrington was playing exceptionally well. He had played his way late into the side with a couple of second-place finishes in recent weeks, so was a ready-made foursomes alternative should Olazábal not be able to sort out his driving.

Even at this early stage, it was clear that Jean Van de Velde, Jarmo Sandelin and Andrew Coltart were to be kept in waiting for the inevitable bad result or loss of form. Van de Velde and Coltart would be neat and tidy foursomes replacements, always nice to have on hand, while Sandelin was more your fourballs man, plenty of birdies mixed in with a few blow-outs.

A quick look at the American team revealed it to be a strong, mature side and one that batted all the way down. In all there were ten who had – or would – win major championships, and only David Duval had not played in a Ryder Cup before. This was the best and most experienced American team to take the field for some time. With home advantage, despite having lost the last two encounters, the United States were unquestionably favourites to win.

Ben Crenshaw was Mark James's opposite number, but not all his players were in the sort of form he would have liked: 'Only perhaps eight or nine were on top of their game going into the match,' recalls Crenshaw.

'Mark O'Meara wasn't playing that well, nor Steve Pate, one of my picks. Davis Love was playing well but was bothered by his putting, so too was Payne Stewart.' Unusually for an American captain, Crenshaw didn't give either O'Meara or Pate a game that first day, even though the first morning America only won one game and halved another. Not for Crenshaw the usual American way of giving everyone a game both the first couple of days.

The Scottish pairing of Montgomerie and Lawrie duly went first in the morning foursomes and having decided that Lawrie should drive the odds, it fell to him to hit the first tee shot, something few rookies have ever had to do. The Open Champion was up to the task and a fine drive set the pattern of their play that morning. Against David Duval and Phil Mickelson the opening five holes were halved, and though the Americans drew first blood, the match was square by the turn and the Scots, who never dropped a shot that morning – quite something in foursomes – drew away to win by 3/2.

Behind them, Parnevik and Garcia had the daunting task of facing Tiger Woods and Tom Lehman. With his first couple of pairings Crenshaw was clearly looking to get some blue (the US colour) on the board early. This they did when Lehman chipped in at the 1st and then went further ahead at the 5th. That was as far as they got, as the two Europeans won the next couple of holes, went ahead at the 12th, and a three at 17 saw them close out the match. Winning those top two games was a dream start.

Behind, Harrington had been substituted for Olazábal, whose driving was not up to it, but he and Jiménez quickly fell behind to a fast start by Love and Stewart. Once again, the Europeans – showing their relish for the pressure cooker that is the Ryder Cup – fought back and did well to pick up half a point by the end of the morning. Only Westwood and Clarke lost, but that was no disgrace as Hal Sutton and Jeff Maggert needed two pars for a 66 when they won by 3/2 – and remember, once again this was foursomes.

The first series of matches are always important and to come out of them ahead by 2½ to 1½ was a fine start. Of great encouragement to Mark James was how well his inexperienced team was playing. Apart from putting Olazábal back in for the fourballs in place of Harrington, there really was no need for any changes. The big game of the afternoon was Westwood and Clarke versus Duval and Woods and there was never more than a hole in it. Birdies were thrown by both sides, but in the end the vital one was that of Clarke at the 17th to go 1 up. A half at the 18th secured a fine victory and it meant that neither Duval nor Woods had any points to show for their day's work.

Elsewhere, only Montgomerie and Lawrie failed to win, halving their match against Love and Justin Leonard. Garcia showed what a great force he would become in the Ryder Cup by winning again with Parnevik, and Olazábal's somewhat erratic driving did nothing to stop him and Jiménez winning as well. To describe a European lead of 6 points to 2 at the end of the first day as a dream start was almost an understatement.

The only sour note was verbal abuse starting to be aimed at Colin Montgomerie. It was only a couple of years after he had become a target of dissident elements in America as a result of overreaction to chiding at the US Open Championship at Congressional. Since then galleries in the United States had seen him as fair game, knowing he could be made to react to goading under stressful circumstances. It was a taste of what would become much more hostile over the weekend.

James now had a dilemma that no European captain had faced before. He had four pairings, and nine players if you include the Harrington/Olazábal split partnership with Jiménez, all playing well and winning points. Only one game had been lost that day and with such a young team, Montgomerie being the oldest at 36, there was no question of anyone needing to be rested before the singles.

There was no partnership you would want to break up (why break the spell?) and to sit out say, Clarke and Westwood, who had been the only pair to lose a foursomes but had redeemed themselves in such fine fashion against Duval and Woods, seemed madness just to give Van de Velde and Coltart a game. There was still the afternoon fourballs, which, after all, would be the much better format to give the others their solitary run. At least they would be hitting their own ball all the way round.

The fates then conspired against James. That second morning play was suspended for half an hour by heavy rain. The captains still had to have their afternoon pairings in by 11.45 AM and with Europe ahead in two and no worse than all square in the others, his dilemma deepened over whether to bring in those who were yet to have a game. Parnevik had indicated he might not want to play in every series, but as he and Garcia were on their way to their 3rd point out of 3, he was more than ready to carry on. Once again, everyone was playing too well to be dropped.

As it transpired two games were lost, Monty and Lawrie and Jiménez and Harrington both losing on the

18th green, but both were matches the Americans won with birdies close home, rather than Europe losing them. One of the winning US pairs was the unlikely combination of Woods and Steve Pate, Pate not having played the first day at all. 'Tiger is hard to find someone to pair him with', said Crenshaw. 'There's no one really with comparable skills, and I don't think any captain has found the answer yet. But that week I discovered Tiger grew up in California with Steve's brother, so he and Steve were already quite friendly. So I put them together and they got us a point.'

James felt the unenviable task of telling Van de Velde, Coltart and Sandelin they were not going to play before the singles was better than trying to guess which of the successful partnerships would be best to stand down. Golfers are enormously aware of that fickle, fragile beast momentum. You mess with it at your peril and Europe undoubtedly had momentum going into the last series of fourballs that afternoon: better to leave well alone.

So out they went again, the order slightly shuffled so as not to make it easy for the Americans to guess who would be playing where. Monty and Lawrie had led the way the first three times, now they went last and drew the successful Woods and Pate. Crenshaw had similar problems to James in that he didn't know how the morning games were going to pan out and neither player from his other successful group in the morning, Sutton and Maggert, got a chance to do it again in the afternoon.

James was now aware that, young as his team were, he was asking a lot of the seven who were now going to have to play in all five series of matches. Every match over those first two days went at least to the 16th green, and several went all the way. James, from his own experiences, knew the almost unique stresses and strains the Ryder Cup can impose on a player (he can remember being almost unable to move when standing over an important putt in the 1989 match). On top of which, play was painfully slow. There had been that rain delay in the morning, and with the fourballs taking well over five hours, most were out there in the heat of battle literally from dawn to dusk, with only a short break for lunch. A contributing factor to the snail's pace was that far more people were getting in to watch than should have been allowed. Even at The Belfry, where there is plenty of room to move around, the crowd is limited to 25,000, those in charge recognising that, with only four matches on the go at any one time, any more spectators and no one would see anything. At The Country Club, with nowhere near the open spaces of The Belfry, upwards of 30,000 or 35,000 were getting in on Friday and Saturday – a number that would rise to more than 40,000 on the Sunday. Probably 30 to 40 minutes a round were wasted settling these vast hordes down and just getting from greens to tees.

It is easy to point the finger at Mark James and list the things he did wrong or the decisions he could have made before and during the match, which would have led to victory rather than defeat. Pick Langer, not Coltart? How silly, when you already have six newcomers in your team, to add another, when instead you have such a brilliant utility player just waiting in the wings. What chance did the three who didn't play till the Sunday have of winning a point, going cold into the intensity of a Sunday at the Ryder Cup? That and much more could and would be levelled at James in the aftermath of defeat seemingly snatched from the jaws of victory.

But few thought he was wrong on the Saturday evening as he took a 10–6 lead into the final day. None of his players criticised his tactics at the time or afterwards, all saying that whatever the price of achieving that sort of advantage was well worth the risk. After all, James's tactics were only an up-to-date version of how Jacklin had driven his proven winners time and again into battle to get the advantage going into the last day. It was just that Jacklin had only once not given a player a run out before the singles and that was Gordon J. Brand in 1983. And never forget, this was a very good US team. It had been kept firmly penned in its cage by the sheer quality of the golf played against it. Never was that old adage, 'they only played as well as they were allowed to', more apt than at Brookline in 1999. Crenshaw summed it up when he said: 'I think the Europeans are more comfortable with these short matches over 18 holes. They make a mistake and they move on from it; we seem to let it debilitate us for some holes afterwards. They have the ability to bounce back from a mistake; I think they just do a beautiful job of that. I guess it is just the Europeans have a better understanding of playing together.'

If one were looking for a route by which James might have found victory, he could perhaps have sent his tried trusted Scotsmen, Montgomerie and Lawrie, off in the first two games: after all, they had gone first in three out of the four series the first two days. They alone, of those who had played all five games, kept their form in the singles and could have given the lead always so important from those going out first. Choosing Westwood and Clarke didn't work. They are both big men and at the time were not as physically fit as they would be later on in their careers. On this hilly course, in considerable heat and with the time and effort they had put into their matches, they had simply run out of steam. They were not able to give the lead that had been hoped for.

Behind them, James had put the three untried rookies: was it a mistake to put them all together, so high up the draw? Would putting them later have made any difference? Who knows? If they were going to be sacrificial lambs, then they might as well absorb the talents of Mickelson, Woods and Love. The news didn't get any better immediately behind. Parnevik soon fell adrift of Duval and would eventually lose 5/4; near the bottom young Garcia too had little left to give and when Jim Furyk began to hole a few putts he did not have an answer. By mid-afternoon it was clear there would be no point from the young Spaniard.

Crenshaw had sent his top players out first to eat into that considerable lead as quickly as possible, a strategy that worked brilliantly. Within an hour and a half the tops of the giant scoreboards were awash with blue, and not just by the odd hole. Over 18 holes and against this quality of opposition these were leads that would not be reeled in. The US team was out of its cage.

Prior to the start of play that Sunday Crenshaw had given a last press conference and boldly forecast victory. Sounding almost like Martin Luther King, he finished by saying: 'Mark my words. I have a feeling about this thing.' Within minutes rather than hours he was looking like the greatest prophet in history: 'It was no more than a feeling', he recalled some years later. 'I knew our players were playing well, just not putting that good. I felt they were getting to understand the course; they definitely hadn't got the hang of it as quickly as the

Europeans, who perhaps play this quirky old-fashioned type of course more often than we do. We put our stronger players out first, hoping they would get ahead and send the message to those behind that maybe we could do this thing. That's just what they did. They started to hole some putts and it changed the atmosphere.

'I was also attuned to what had happened at The Country Club, at Brookline, all those years ago and in so many matches; not only the 1913 US Open, but Walker Cups, competitions that reached a crescendo and something happened for Americans and American teams playing there. We seemed to have got the breaks and I thought that might just happen again.'

But Europe only had to win 4 points out of 12 that afternoon to retain the trophy and even amidst all that carnage it soon became clear it could still be done. It was also clear who would have to do it. Padraig Harrington in match 7 would be the first really to get into a game and make a fist of it, the top half dozen games already being lost causes.

Against O'Meara, only a year past his two major championship victories, Harrington got into just the sort of scrap he really enjoys – holes going back and forth and never much in it. It says a lot for his character that, with all the horrors going on ahead, American roars echoing from all parts and the realisation how important his point would be, he played his game and hunted O'Meara home. All square playing the last, Harrington hit a fine drive and got his second to 10 feet. In the end, he was afforded the luxury of two putts for the hole as O'Meara made a mess of it.

Immediately behind Harrington, Jiménez was having quite a tussle with Steve Pate – neither the prettiest of golfers – but both effective. It was a match that Jiménez never led, but he was never so far back that he might not turn it around. But about the time Harrington was seeing off O'Meara, Jiménez succumbed on the 17th green. Now the arithmetic was clear: Olazábal and Montgomerie both had to win, as did Paul Lawrie, at the time 4 up through the turn in the final game against Jeff Maggert. If so, Europe could still tie the match and keep the Cup.

Olazábal was also 4 up through the turn against Justin Leonard. Then Leonard got on one of his putting streaks and started to claw his way back. Up till now the vast crowd had been noisy but largely well behaved. There were far too many for any to be able to follow a given match, they just had to stay where they were and watch the games come through. Beer was on hand and progress could be followed on the scoreboards. As the possibility of a famous recovery loomed, the sound increased in volume and became almost feral. Those who had seen the matches through the early holes now surged towards the finish, swelling the already dense numbers there.

As Leonard reeled Olazábal in with one great putt after another – and we are not talking 5- or 6-footers here – everyone could hear his progress from the thousands who could see it. Like some giant long-drawn-out echo, the roar would then be repeated as the result would materialise on the great boards further down the course. Just the sheer volume of so many people jammed in such a small space gave The Country Club the atmosphere of a vast outdoor arena set up for a world championship fight.

Another long putt snaked in across the 16th green and Leonard was level. Olazábal hadn't dropped a shot, but he'd lost four holes out of six in a match everyone knew he had to win. Both found the 17th green in two, the green where Ouimet had finally seen off Vardon and Ray all those years ago. Olazábal was marginally the closer in two, but neither with a realistic chance of a three. Both would have been happy with two putts and move to the last all square. But Leonard had one more unbelievable putt in his locker: up the slopes it climbed and straight into the hole, and then all hell broke loose.

Most of the Americans who had finished were there, all pretty high on the adrenaline of their own perform- ances, and unquestionably roused by sheer ferocity of the sound around them – a noise certainly greater than they would have heard on any golf course ever. They also believed – because that was the information com- ing over on the closed-circuit radios in the crowd – that Leonard's putt would finally put the match beyond the reach of the Europeans; when it went in, they all thought that was that, the match had been won. A moment's sanity and they would have realised that Olazábal still had a putt for the half and could still win at the 18th. But there was little sanity at that moment or in that place. The stampede by the American players across that 17th green forever turned a famous and courageous fightback into a dreadful, unforgivable breach of etiquette and conduct – one they would singly and collectively regret for the rest of their days. Such a pity, because they had all done such a wonderful job to get to that position in the first place: 'You know, had that putt of Justin's been holeable, say 10 or 15 feet, then I don't think the reaction would have been the same', reflects Crenshaw. 'But it was just so improb- able, so extraordinary, and we just completely lost our

minds; we all lost them – I did. Our emotions completely got the better of us. It was all so highly improbable.
But you know, there was no excuse for it, and there is
no question that it is a lifelong regret.'

Far worse in many respects was the treatment meted
out to Montgomerie throughout the three days. The
abuse continued and got worse the longer the week
went on, and on that last day it turned from verbal to
physical. He was jostled and spat on as he passed
through crowds too vast to be kept back for the passage
of players. It was an attack on a single player the like of
which has never been perpetrated on a golfer in the
pursuit of his profession. Far worse than the momen-
tary loss of sanity by the players, the collective behaviour of the Boston crowd that week against one man left
the sourest taste of all.

CHAPTER NINE

The Walker Cup

1999 and 2001
Peter McEvoy

Certainly, *The Captain's Challenge* is about the way various captains changed our fortunes in the Ryder Cup after decades of American domination, but it would be wrong to ignore what was happening in the amateur game at the same time. The Walker Cup had more or less followed the same sad path as its professional counterpart: 70 years or so of US superiority interspersed by the occasional, out-of-the-blue victory just to keep the myth alive that this really was a serious contest. But by the end of the 1990s, achievements in the Walker Cup, particularly under the captaincy of Peter McEvoy, were to have some bearing on the European Ryder Cup teams of the early 21st century.

Both Ryder and Walker Cup matches started around the same time, the mid-1920s, and both became formalised into biennial contests for a challenge trophy, only after informal matches had sparked the idea in the first place. Samuel Ryder from Hertfordshire gave the trophy that bears his name, while George Walker, grandfather and great-grandfather of the two Presidents Bush, came up with its amateur equivalent.

In the immediate post-war years the US amateur ranks were filled with phenomenal golfers – the likes of Charlie Coe, Don Cherry, Billy Jo Patton, Dick Chapman, Frank Stranahan and Harvie Ward – who were arguably as good as their professional counter-parts and almost as well known. They also played as much golf, several wintering in and round Palm Beach, and spending their summers competing in the many amateur events around the United States. It was only after Arnold Palmer beat 41-year-old New York socialite, Bobby Sweeney, 1 up in the final of the 1954 US Amateur Championship – and then went on to elevate the professional game to unforeseen levels – that one felt golf's baton pass irrevocably from the amateur to the professional.

These great amateurs were the heirs of Bobby Jones, the man who dreamt up the concept of a Grand Slam and then achieved his version of it, winning the Open and Amateur Championships of Great Britain and the United States in a single year, 1930. Right from the start of the Walker Cup our best players were constantly up against seriously good full-time golfers. Most of our players were true amateurs, holding down proper jobs and playing golf only at weekends. There was no escaping to the sun between November and April, and winter golf consisted of good club competition or matches against undergraduates from Oxford and Cambridge. If you were lucky, there would be golf at the seaside, links courses often being at their best in the winter – no preferred lies and firm fast greens.

Thus the Walker Cup wasn't a fair contest and the US quickly racked up a series of quick and one-sided victories. The one exception was at St Andrews in 1938. Henry Cotton was the biggest name in golf at the time, having won the 1937 Open Championship at Carnoustie, against the full might of that year's US Ryder Cup team. The week of the Walker Cup Cotton was at St Andrews and was invited to play with our team in practice. News of his presence quickly spread and huge crowds came out to watch, virtually all following Cotton and the British team. For once the Americans were totally ignored. What part Cotton's presence played in Great Britain and Ireland's narrow victory that weekend can only be guessed at, but it was often mentioned as a significant factor.

In the 1960s the format was changed from one day of 36-hole foursomes and one of singles, to 18-hole foursomes and singles each day: the theory being that over 18 holes the underdogs – us – might have a better chance of springing a surprise. We should have won in 1965, in the US, having gained a 5-point lead with only the eight singles to come, but in the end Clive Clark had to hole a 30-footer on the final green to halve his match, and the overall contest. The enormity of what they were about to achieve may have tripped the Great Britain and Ireland team up at the last hurdle. It was a classic case of not expecting to do that well and unable to seize the prize when it was on offer.

Victory did come in 1971, for no particular reason, this time with a stunning last afternoon resurgence, when we won six of the last eight singles. Here we were going down to another predictable defeat. Possibly everyone relaxed and played their normal game; the

Americans also relaxed, in anticipation of another easy win, but suddenly a most unexpected victory was snatched from the jaws of defeat – by us for once, instead of the other way round!

It would be another eighteen years before we would win again, and the first time ever in the United States. If you were to look for something out of the ordinary that might have helped, in February of that year – 1989 – Russell Claydon, an amateur from Gog Ma Gog in Cambridge, almost won the Australian Masters from a good field that included Greg Norman. In the end, only Norman would finish in front of him and Claydon hounded the Great White Shark right to the line. He was by no means the dominant player in the Great Britain and Ireland team and his peers would have looked at that performance and thought, 'well I've beaten him as often as he has beaten me, so I must be pretty good too.'

By this time, the matches were undoubtedly becoming closer. The professional game had sufficient rewards to attract the young and gifted, so many more were coming through the amateur ranks. Also, some of our best young players were now going to college in the States, by some way the best set of nursery slopes for anyone considering playing the game for a living. The competition for places on those college teams is intense, every week there are medal matches against other universities, northern colleges have southern bases, so the game can be played continuously in ideal conditions. By the time you head for the qualifying school for the professional tour, you are a hardened competitor, and that camel-through-the-eye-of-a-needle examination seems a relatively benign affair.

Tiger Woods played his only Walker Cup in 1995 at

Porthcawl in Wales, but his defeat on the first afternoon in the singles at the hands of Gary Wolstenholme was somehow a turning point and Great Britain and Ireland completed a fine victory the following day. David Howell and Padraig Harrington have gone on to greater things and in retrospect that side was a pretty good one. As a matter of interest, Woods remains the only American ever to have been on losing sides in Walker, Ryder and President Cup Matches – a detail I don't suppose will bother him much as he marches to his destiny, but nice to mention amidst the eulogies his record usually produces.

The year 1997 saw a disappointing return to the underperformance of what had looked a good Great Britain and Ireland side on paper. Justin Rose was there, less than a year before he was to burst on the scene with that holed pitch at the 72nd hole in the Open Championship; so too Gary Wolstenholme, by now a tried-and-tested Walker Cup player and with wins in the Amateur Championship, building a reputation to intimidate young college kids on their first Walker Cup outing.

For years American teams always seemed to include crusty old players with long successful careers in the amateur game. In the 1960s and 1970s you had the likes of Bill Campbell, Bill Hyndman and Ed Tutweiller: all well into their 40s and sometimes their 50s, still playing lots of competitive golf and still well able to look after themselves. Following them came Jay Sigel and Allen Doyle in the 1990s. These were all tough nuts for a young first-time Great Britain and Ireland player to come up against. The days of these stalwarts playing nine holes in 29 were probably past, but they knew how to win, had formidable records and made few mistakes.

They were also intimidating opponents. Gary Wolstenholme was just about the first on our side ever to assume this role against them. He played his first Walker Cup match in 1995 and several more over the next decade.

Then, in 1998, the Royal and Ancient appointed Peter McEvoy as captain for the match at Nairn the following year. McEvoy had twice won the Amateur Championship in 1977 and 1978, played several times in the Walker Cup, including that first ever victory in America in 1989, but his crowning achievement was to lead Great Britain and Ireland to victory in the 1988 Eisenhower Trophy, which was for four-man teams from each nation and played every four years. Once again this was an international competition that had largely been the preserve of the Americans, and that year, only McEvoy stood between them and another USA victory. He had to keep ahead of a couple of the US players throughout the final nine holes: this he did and ground out a famous victory, in the process taking the individual title as well.

With his record, it was only a question of time before the captaincy would come his way. As a player, while by no means the most stylish, he had supreme confidence in his ability and, in life, absolute certainty that whatever route he chose, it would be the right one. His ability to see what he wanted to do and then do it was reminiscent of a young Tony Jacklin. Having established what it was they wanted, neither had any doubts they had what it took to succeed: 'Once I was past my middle 20s, I was always going to be an amateur,' Peter now recalls, 'and obviously after the playing career, the next thing was to be captain. So, I paid a lot of attention while I was playing and I looked forward to it. You have to wait for these things to come along, but when it did, I was ready for it. I had my own ideas as to what I wanted to do.

'I was England captain first and in some ways was even more successful than in the Walker Cup. England won five Home Internationals in a row, something never done before or since. So I was able to try out what I thought important and refine things as I went along. With what I achieved with the England team, I knew I was on the right lines.

'I read a lot – business books and military history – always with an idea on gleaning what I could for the day I would have teams to lead. In all these books there was something about leadership and of course captaincy is a form of leadership. I blended that with the experience of playing under various captains. You hang on the good bits and discard the rubbish. I played under a few good captains, and several dreadful ones, but I learnt something from all of them.'

Having played on several losing Walker Cup teams, as well as being part of the team that won for the first time ever on US soil, McEvoy was well aware of the barriers to be overcome if all players on his teams were to play their best when it mattered. Successive generations of British Walker Cup teams had gone into the match in awe of the reputations of their opponents and intimidated by the sheer weight of history: 36 matches played and less than a handful of victories to show for it: 'The number of players I've spoken to over the years who've said more or less the same thing. "If only I'd known they (the Americans) would be as ordinary as that, I'd have gone in with a totally different approach." So my main task was to get that approach before the match rather than after it. I had to change people's expectations of what they could achieve in the match. We had the players – we've often had the players – but very few ever believed we could do well, that winning was a possibility.

'I knew the problem, but even the reading of books didn't give me the whole answer. So, I went to Saatchi & Saatchi, where Adam Crozier was MD, after stints at the Football Association and Royal Mail. I knew that all sorts of people went to ad agencies with problems, and if they didn't know the answer, they might know someone who would. I told Adam, "we have a bunch of really good players but we are going into a match not expecting to win."

'His people were brilliant, instantly understood the problem, and we produced a video; just a two- or three-minute piece. It was of an anonymous Walker Cup player, who'd just been picked, and instead of highlighting the enormity of our task, concentrated on the size of the problem facing the Americans with the team we had – winners of seven out of the last eight European Team Championships, a team with the two best US college players in Luke Donald and Paul Casey and others who had won our Amateur Championship and sundry other championships around the world. At the end, this new Walker Cup player knocked an iron stiff at the last, shook hands and then walked off across the greenside lake! It was a simple thing, but I know it worked as Philip Rowe, the youngest player on our side in 1999, played it over and over again in the run up to the match.

'From my own playing days I remembered the damaging effects of negative thinking. In 1977, having won the Amateur Championship, I was qualified to play in the NEC World Series at Akron, Ohio. They kept changing the qualification rules, but back then it was only a field of 22, mostly the winners of the major championships and other multiple winners of tournaments, plus the Amateur Champions of the US and Great Britain. To be honest, I was the only person I'd never heard of! In such company I had the most hideous negative expectations; I was just [determined] not to embarrass myself.

'A year or so later, on the 11th tee in the final round of the Open at Lytham, I was four shots off the lead, and lying in 4th place. I dropped a couple of shots coming in, finished 17th. Now, if I'd had that experience behind me, I'd have gone to Akron in an entirely different frame of mind and I am sure, done much better. So, with each member of the team I concentrated on what they had achieved, the golf they had played just to get into the side that made them more than qualified to be in the team, and with golf that was quite good enough to do well in the match and win games.

'From my military history books, I learnt that groups of people can sometimes achieve more collectively than they might if going about a task individually; that the whole can be greater than the sum of the parts. The most important thing is to show any team, particularly if you are a non-playing captain, that you are part of that team. I have played under several captains who couldn't get into that role, were somehow aloof; captains who would see you off the 1st tee and then you don't see them again until the match is over. They just don't think there is anything they can do once the team is out on the course. But that's not true.

'To start with, I have always believed the captain has to be the spokesman for the team with the media. It is not as big, anywhere near, as in the Ryder Cup, but it is there and it has grown over the years. If you are not used to it, all that spotlight stuff can be a bit intimidating, and I believed that was for me to take as far as possible.

'Both at Nairn [1999] and at Sea Island, Georgia [2001], we were seen to have good sides, ones with a very good chance of winning, but in both at the end of the first day we were losing. I saw this as a good opportunity. If you are down you have to get the press on your side. You have to talk the team up to them, and this is a big way you can show the players you are on their side, are part of the team and be prepared publicly to show your belief in them. At Nairn, the press were quite aggressive. "Here! You said this was a great team, and here we are losing again, just as usual." I had to convince them I still thought we had a good team, and that we would win. I really went in to bat for them, said it was the worst result we could have had, and that we could turn the thing round the following day; which we did!

'I let the team know what was being said about them, but that I had backed them to the hilt, that I definitely thought we could turn it round on day two. As I say, I saw this as an opportunity to show that I could do something for them, stand up for them, put myself on the line.

'You always have to be honest, particularly when you have made a mistake, and I made plenty. When you've got it wrong, a bit of humility, a bit of frailty can often turn a negative into a positive. At Sea Island in 2001, again a poor first day, but in the morning Jamie Elson and Richard McEvoy [no relation] had done heroics coming back from 3 down and three to play to halve. In the euphoria of the moment I told them that with that comeback they had both earned their berth in the singles the following day – neither were playing that afternoon's singles, as only eight out of the ten play at any one time.

'As it turned out, the singles went poorly that after-

noon and we were behind overnight. Obviously needing our best players both morning and afternoon, I
found I really couldn't play both of them in the singles
the following day – remember, in the Walker Cup the
line-up for both morning and afternoon has to be put
in the night before. I was mindful that I was going to
make either Jamie or Richard very disappointed, maybe
ruin their confidence, as both were obviously playing
together again in the foursomes. In announcing the
team that evening, I made out what an idiot I had been
to promise something I couldn't deliver – took all the
blame – but said it was just because everyone was playing so well, one of them had to stand down, and it was
Richard. They still delivered a foursomes point the following day and Jamie halved his singles. We won that
final singles 6½–1½.'

Clearly Peter McEvoy put a tremendous amount of
time, energy and thought into his years as captain. Ally
that with his passion to win, his air of supreme confidence and his deep insight into how to blend a bunch
of individual players into a team, and you probably have
a captain the equal of most, if not all, of those who have
done the job so well in the Ryder Cup. It should also be
remembered that in the Walker Cup it has always been
just Great Britain and Ireland versus America (no help
from Europe) and with the rewards in the professional
game, very few amateurs stay for more than one Walker
Cup. Thus he was fortunate to have had not just the
rock that is Gary Wolstenholme, but Luke Donald as
well for both his campaigns.

In both 1999 and 2001 McEvoy had to rally his side
after falling behind on the first day, and in some ways
the better the job he had done in creating the team and
its self-belief, the harder the task of getting it back up

after the shock of not being ahead at the halfway stage. Even to this day, his stock reference to those disappointing opening days is, '6½–5½ is the worst it could have been,' at Nairn, or at Sea Island, 'it just went wrong at the end; we'd outplayed them for most of the day.' And that was the message he took into the team room. Confidence, belief in them, no contemplation that they might just be up against a better side. As was the case with Tony Jacklin, and of course Seve, losing just wasn't an option.

At Nairn, Great Britain and Ireland were still behind going into the singles on the second day, but all went right in the afternoon: 'I was very lucky that second day, as I made a decision for one reason that worked for a totally different one. We had three Scots in the team, but that first day two of them, Lorne Kelly and David Patrick, were right off their game. The third, Graham Rankin, a past winner of the Amateur Championship, had not played well in the World Cup, lost both the games he played in 1997 at Quaker Ridge, and lost both matches here on the first day.

'Now I was going to have a problem in Scotland leaving out two Scots, and I wasn't particularly hopeful of getting anything from Graham either. I thought the best use I could make of him was to send him out early, take the bulk of the home crowd with him and hope to get some cheers echoing round the place early. I told him that we were losing, that we needed to get this thing going our way early and that I thought he was the chap to take the home crowd with him, so was putting him out top in both foursomes and singles.

'He was transformed. He'd been given a specific job to do, given responsibility by his captain, and instead of being hidden away down the order, was out there at the top. He really came out fighting, played heroically and won both his matches. Unquestionably his performance at the top was an inspiration to the team, and that last afternoon we won seven out of the eight singles. It was a lesson for me how different people respond to different messages. If he hadn't been a Scot, I would probably have tucked him away in the middle of the pack and got nothing from him.'

Honesty, lack of false modesty, a willingness to learn from mistakes and turn negatives into positives, has been at the heart of McEvoy's years of captaincy. He clearly found the challenges, both personal and intellectual, fascinating and when it came to his last stint, at Sea Island in 2001, he put what was by now a wealth of experience into getting it just right: 'I thought our preparation for that match was spot on. We met at the Gatwick hotel on the Saturday morning (the match starting exactly a week later), and that afternoon caught the train to Victoria and went to Buckingham Palace for a reception. We took taxis from the station and drove in through the gates of the Palace, past the crowds. This had been organised by Peter Dawson, Secretary of the Royal and Ancient, through the Duke of York, who had been captain of the Royal and Ancient the year before. His Royal Highness was there to meet us and we had tea in that large room with the balconies overlooking the Mall.

'Why go to all the bother? This was all about making them feel good about themselves, recognising they were something special. There they were in their blazers and ties, in a special place with special people. The following day on the plane, club-class travel and team introductions from the captain – all little things in themselves, but all part of team building.

'When we got to America we didn't go straight to Sea Island, we went to Hilton Head instead. We were in the United States acclimatising, but not getting to the course too early. I remember playing in the match at Shinnecock in 1977; we got there something like ten days before the start – way too long. Two practice rounds, three at most, and you are ready to play the match, but it is still three or four days away. The adrenaline dries up, the passion evaporates. I was determined not to make that mistake.

'In fact the American team did just that. By the time the match started they had been there a week. They started off playing twice a day in the fierce heat, then after a couple of days they started looking for difficulties. They started doing things individually: one evening the wind sprang up from a different direction, so some went out to play the final holes into that wind; others went out and played west-running holes to practise playing into the setting sun. They even went looking for bunkers they hadn't been in just to hit shots out of them in case they did. They may have been a team at the start, but by the time we got there on the Tuesday, they were a bunch of individuals out looking for problems.

'We stayed a couple of days at Hilton Head, playing in those very hot conditions and on courses of similar composition to the one at Sea Island. They were all working on their games, getting acclimatised, but not yet at Sea Island. Even when we got there on the Tuesday I wouldn't let them out on the course itself; we played one of the other ones. So by the time they set foot on the Ocean Course, they were like greyhounds let off the leash.

'By this time the Americans were all out doing their own thing and the contrast was extreme; we'd been together for some three or four days and I felt we really were a team. A good example was when the match got underway. After losing the foursomes, the USA had a very good finish to the singles, turning round matches that had looked good for us early on. With one game left out, and the scores level, play was suspended by a thunderstorm for about an hour. Michael Hoey was 2 down and two to play, but when they restarted all our lads were out there – without a word from me – and not one American player was there to support their man. Michael won the 17th, but sadly made a mess of 18, so there was no fairy tale finish.'

The contrast in team spirit was matched by the contrast between captains. McEvoy's opposite number, both at Nairn and Sea Island, was Danny Yates, a member of a Southern golfing dynasty. His uncle Charlie had been on a couple of American teams before the war and his father had been hugely instrumental in helping rebuild East Lake in Atlanta, the course where Bobby Jones grew up and which had fallen into total disrepair when the demographics of Atlanta shifted. They were an Atlanta family through and through.

Danny Yates himself had also played on a couple of American teams, the losing one at Peachtree, in Atlanta, in 1989 and a winning one at Interlaken in 1993. In fact, he even played Peter McEvoy twice in singles at Peachtree, winning and losing one apiece. But he was the total opposite of McEvoy. Somewhat aloof and very much hands off, he was probably rather shy and one felt he would rather be playing than captaining. He preferred to play in practice with his teams as opposed to bustling around getting things sorted and he seemed to have the Jack Nicklaus approach to captaincy – his boys knew how to prepare for competition, his job was to pick the colours for the day and put in the pairings. Against McEvoy that approach just didn't work.

As at Nairn, that second day started well for Great Britain and Ireland, up in three and down in one, a position that would be maintained to the end. And wherever there seemed to be a crucial point in a match, there was the slightly stout, reassuring figure of McEvoy – no rushing about like Seve – just there, calm, impressive and somehow with just the right word to the right individual: 'Once the games got underway, and I had seen everyone off the 1st tee, I would make my way to a short hole which the top match was about to reach. You are out there trying to help and I saw my role to give encouragement; talk about how the match is going, look for positives in what has happened so far. I particularly go to a par-3 because I can see what club they have taken, and when the next group comes through I can pass that on to our player; also how the ball reacted in the wind. Just little bits of inside information.

'I would also pass on any good news – Gary's 3 up, or Graham's just got back to all square – all part of making them feel part of it; particularly in the singles, when you can feel a bit out there on your own. I usually go from par-3 to par-3. Everyone plays the shot from the same place, so it's the same test, and for those coming behind, you've always got some information that's useful. As we get towards the end, I look for those matches that are close, one up or all square, games that are going be important, and head there. Talking of Danny Yates, he always seemed to be with the match where the Americans were 6 up; I could never see the point of that.'

2001 ended the same way as 1999, with Great Britain and Ireland sailing away into the sunset. They won six of the final eight singles, halved one and lost the other, and for the first time in the history of the Walker Cup Great Britain and Ireland had won two consecutive matches, and three out of the last four. As is the way with the Royal and Ancient, that would be the end of Peter McEvoy's reign as captain: no begging him to stay on and work the miracle once again. But he was not finished with the match. After captaincy comes a stint as Chairman of Selectors, a role he took to with his usual thoroughness and detailed planning. And at Ganton two years later he was part of the mix that brought the trophy home for a third consecutive time: 'Do you know, one of my greatest moments came when I heard the USGA had set up a committee to try and work out why they were suddenly doing so badly in the Walker Cup! You look at their preparation now and they are doing all the things we were doing – not getting to the venue too early – that sort of thing. That's why they are getting harder to beat again.'

Somewhere, though, there must now be a blueprint, a guide for future captains, somewhere within the Royal and Ancient, so that all that Peter McEvoy brought to the job can be used by those who follow. And from those teams, nearly a decade ago now, Padraig Harrington, David Howell, Luke Donald and Paul Casey have all come from successful Walker Cup teams to make their contribution in the Ryder Cup. Nick Dougherty and Simon Dyson look sure to follow in their footsteps. The Americans, whether professional or amateur, are no longer the all-conquering superstars they once were.

The Belfry

27–29 September

Europe (*Sam Torrance*)	Matches		USA (*Curtis Strange*)

Fourballs: *Morning*

D. Clarke & T. Björn (1 hole)	1	0	T. Woods & P. Azinger
S. Garcia & L. Westwood (4/3)	1	0	D. Duval & D. Love III
C. Montgomerie & B. Langer (4/3)	1	0	S. Hoch & J. Furyk
P. Harrington & N. Fasth	0	1	P. Mickelson & D. Toms (1 hole)

Foursomes: *Afternoon*

D. Clarke & T. Björn	0	1	H. Sutton & S. Verplank (2/1)
S. Garcia & L. Westwood (2/1)	1	0	T. Woods & M. Calcavecchia
C. Montgomerie & B. Langer (halved)	½	½	P. Mickelson & D. Toms (halved)
P. Harrington & P. McGinley	0	1	S. Cink & J. Furyk (3/2)

Foursomes: *Morning*

P. Fulke & P. Price	0	1	P. Mickelson & D. Toms (2/1)
L. Westwood & S. Garcia (2/1)	1	0	S. Cink & J. Furyk
C. Montgomerie & B. Langer (1 hole)	1	0	S. Verplank & S. Hoch
D. Clarke & T. Björn	0	1	T. Woods & D. Love III (4/3)

Fourballs: *Afternoon*

N. Fasth & J. Parnevik	0	1	M. Calcavecchia & D. Duval (1 hole)
C. Montgomerie & P. Harrington (2/1)	1	0	P. Mickelson & D. Toms
S. Garcia & L. Westwood	0	1	T. Woods & D. Love III (1 hole)
D. Clarke & P. McGinley (halved)	½	½	S. Hoch & J. Furyk (halved)

Singles

C. Montgomerie (5/4)	1	0	S. Hoch
S. Garcia	0	1	D. Toms (1 hole)
D. Clarke (halved)	½	½	D. Duval (halved)
B. Langer (4/3)	1	0	H. Sutton
P. Harrington (5/4)	1	0	M. Calcavecchia
T. Björn (2/1)	1	0	S. Cink
L. Westwood	0	1	S. Verplank (2/1)
N. Fasth (halved)	½	½	P. Azinger (halved)
P. McGinley (halved)	½	½	J. Furyk (halved)
P. Fulke (halved)	½	½	D. Love III (halved)
P. Price (3/2)	1	0	P. Mickelson
J. Parnevik (halved)	½	½	T. Woods (halved)

Europe	15½	12½	USA

CHAPTER TEN

An Extra Year to Prepare

2002
Sam Torrance

After the unseemly scuffles at Brookline in 1999, Sam Torrance might not have seemed quite the most emollient choice as captain for the next match at The Belfry two years later. But the feisty and sometimes rambunctious Scot is a man of pride as well as passion, and was determined that an event that had played such a big part in his own life must immediately be restored to its former stature. Also, the match was played three years later, in 2002, because of 9/11, and that in itself ensured an entirely different atmosphere when Europe and America came together once again: 'I was lucky in that their captain was Curtis Strange. We took about three seconds to agree that there wasn't going to be a repeat of Brookline. He and his delightful wife Sarah were the most I could have wished for as opposition that particular week.

'In some ways Brookline helped form my priorities. I determined that excellence was to be the byword. I wanted everything to be perfect for the team; I wanted the course to be perfect, the clothing, food, the rooms, everything perfect. I wanted not one minor hitch, and if a player wanted anything, I wanted to be able to provide it.

'I was lucky, of course, to have that extra year to get everything right', Sam reflected. Some captains might have been fazed by the hiatus. What happens if some of the players lose form? How will those playing for the first time cope with a whole year to think about it? But Torrance saw only positives: 'Captains usually only have three or four weeks with their final team; yes they will know who eight or nine of them are, but often there are places to be played for right up to the time when the team is announced. Then they have to turn them into a team, with so little time and all the uniforms and team colours to be sorted out; pairings to be thought about, that sort of thing. I had a whole year; what a luxury.

'You have no idea how many things there are to be done. I had been lucky to be Mark James' deputy at Brookline. There had been a chance, when Mark was appointed captain in 1998, I would be in the team. I had won the French Open that year, but didn't make the side and Mark had said if I wasn't playing he would want me to help him. It was a blessing, it taught me so much more than if I had been playing. As a player you only have to think about your own game and the match; you expect most things to be sorted out by others, but until you are on the support staff, you have no idea how much there is going on behind the scenes.

'It was good for the players too. They obviously knew that whole year they were in the team, so could plan their schedule, be fit and fresh for the big day. How often have two or three had to struggle through July and August to scrape together the points just to make the side, and then have little left for the match itself?

'Then we had the chance to get together as a team at The Belfry on a couple of occasions. We were missing Sergio Garcia and Jesper Parnevick , who were playing in America, but the other ten were there.

'I had Jesse [Mark James] and Woosie [Ian Woosnam] as my deputies, and they played, so we were like a proper team. Even then there was great excitement, just being there; nothing like the Ryder Cup, of course, but it gave the rookies a little taste of what was to come.

'Not everyone was playing well. I remember the last afternoon and I put Pierre Fulke and Philip Price against Jesse and Woosie. They weren't playing well, and were quite down about it. Now I wouldn't put them out against the two stand-ins without saying anything, so I said to Fulke, "you're game's a bit off and I want you show me something – a bit of determination – show me what you've got." I didn't say it to Phil, it might have had the reverse effect, broken him a bit. Anyway, it worked. They had the best score of the lot that afternoon.'

Just that little tale showed the thought and insight Torrance brought to the job – and not a little psychology as well. Some had thought he might bring a rather gung-ho approach to the job of captaincy, treat it all as a bit of a lark, good time out with the boys. They could not have been more wrong. No one has left fewer stones unturned to ensure perfection on the day. He spoke to anyone who he felt could help him get it right. 'I learnt a lot from Sir Alex Ferguson, who said, "The key factor in any team is there are no superstars. You've got to elevate your rookies, anyone who isn't playing that well, and bring down your superstars a bit." All I know is the whole team gelled beautifully.'

But the man who made the most difference to Sam was Professor David Purdy, a gynaecologist from Ayr. Just after Christmas 2000, Sunningdale Golf Club had had its centenary dinner, at which there were three speakers. Sandy Tatum, board member of the United States Golf Association and doyen of the Royal and Ancient, went first, followed by Lord Griffiths QC, past President of the MCC. Both spoke eloquently and excellently, and were daunting acts to follow. But then came David Purdy, of whom few had ever heard. Even for the jaded, after-dinner speech attendees, his performance was the stuff of legend: 'He was quite magnificent,' recalls Torrance, 'and when it was all over I went up to him and said, "You can really help me at the Ryder Cup." To which he replied, "How kind of you to ask, but you do realise I'm only an amateur!" However, the two of them got together to great effect.

The one chink in Torrance's armour was a fear of public speaking: 'I was terrified of public speaking – quite irrational really. I had played in eight Ryder Cups and each time the captain went up to the podium at the opening ceremony to speak to the world: I just thought, thank God it's him not me. I never saw myself as an orator ... more of a heckler, I suppose! I was terrified of messing up. In my mind it was just something I didn't do.

'I went up to David's house in Ayr a few times. In all, we got together five or six times. He was quite brilliant. I had four speeches to make and with his help I got them all written – my words, but he put them in the right order, elegantly. He taught me about pausing, where to look, that sort of thing. Quite a few people know it now, but I had the podium delivered down to my house, the actual one I would have at the opening ceremony, and for a week I practiced for a couple of hours a day; recorded each one, then listened back, recorded again, then listened. Long before I ever got to The Belfry for the match, I had them all memorised, off pat. That was just one more thing I didn't have to worry about that week.'

Something else all captains can do, at least when it's a home match, is prepare the course to suit what they believe to be their team's strengths, much along the lines of a cricket captain deciding whether to use the light or heavy roller. It was another area where attention to detail could reap considerable home bene-fit. 'I thought long and hard about how best to set the course up at The Belfry. I felt their team was longer, man for man, than ours, and they probably played more aggressively. There's less punishment for wild driving in America, so they tend to get the driver out more often, or at least don't have to worry as much as Europeans do about where specifically to put the ball off the tee.

'We put in some new bunkers, further on than the existing ones, narrowed the fairways, particularly from about 290 yards onwards and thickened up the rough. Then all the surrounds to the greens were given a crew-cut; there was to be none of that thick grass just off the putting surface that seems to be the standard defence of greens in the US. Half our team would have been all right, they play over there, but the other half didn't and would have been at a disadvantage.

'Finally, I never wanted the tee moved up at the 10th [a short par-4 over water that became well within reach from one of the forward tees and a regular practice when ordinary tournaments are played there]. They were longer, and it would have been like creating another par-3 with the Americans using shorter clubs than we would. If they wanted to go for the green, then it would have to be with a driver. Keeping the tee back gave them more of a quandary than us. It reached me they were a bit irritated by this; they didn't think it a very good hole where you just hit a 6- or 7-iron off the tee. But anything that irritated them, within the context of the match, was all right by me!'

Although 1999 had been a defeat, and leaving aside all the rabble-rousing for which the match will always be remembered, that contest demonstrated Europe now had a ready supply of players capable of taking on and beating the Americans home or away. We were competitive, even though that great band of major winners from the 1980s were all but gone. Strange to think the only one still in harness was Bernhard Langer, whom most would have picked to be first down, beset as he was throughout his career with the 'twitch'. He was right up there with the best from long distance, but the 2- and 3-footers had always been his Achilles heel. What a tribute to mind over matter!

And by now Langer wasn't just another really good player in a team of good players, he was a trump in a pack of court cards. The bigger the competition, the better he was likely to play, and who better to send out with a first timer, than this calm impressive man, be it in foursome or fourball? Apart from Langer, there were now seasoned Ryder Cup players: Darren Clarke and Lee Westwood (a partnership that had produced so much at Brookline), Sergio Garcia, a Ballesteros-lite maybe, but all the potential in the world, and with all Seve's ability to get right up the noses of the opposition. Then there was Colin Montgomerie, Padraig

Harrington and Thomas Björn. Looking back six or seven years on, what a great young team it was and what a base for the future.

As with so much for this match, Sam Torrance had thought long and hard about his pairings: 'I'd had my pairings done weeks before, at home; remember, this team had been established for a year, so I knew who would be playing. I had the whole week on a piece of paper, Thursday and Friday, morning and afternoon, and even the singles line-up. That was my plan. But I changed it all when I got there! I certainly used some of the pairings but others emerged in practice. Garcia and Westwood – where that came from, I have no idea. They were not on my list and only played nine holes together the last afternoon of practice.

'Westwood came to The Belfry with no form whatsoever; he was playing well enough, but had not put four good rounds together in tournaments for a long time. At some point I took him aside and told him, "look Lee, form is temporary, class is forever. You're hitting the ball well, this course suits you and the odd bad shot only costs one hole"; all that sort of stuff. Anyway, with Garcia he played really well.

'I had decided to break up the Clarke/Westwood partnership, partly because of Lee's form, but also I felt after Brookline where they did so well, that going out again together might be counter-productive; going to that particular well too often. Also, I couldn't put Garcia out again with Jesper Parnevik, as Parnevik had rung me from America saying he just couldn't keep the ball on the planet, and he wouldn't mind if he didn't play till the singles. He was really the only one whom the year's wait hadn't benefited. So perhaps that's where Garcia and Westwood came from.'

Bernhard Langer and Colin Montgomerie was a natural. They had played together five years previously at
Valderrama and won a couple of times. Of course,
Langer had been an omission at Brookline, so it was
certainly not a partnership from which all the juice had
been squeezed. The only criticism you might make is
that with four newcomers in the team, this was like putting two golden eggs in the same basket. Mind you, the
first morning you want to put out all your strength, and
when they keep winning, it is hard to split them.

Those two partnerships – Westwood/Garcia and
Langer/Montgomerie – produced 5½ points of the 8
that Europe were to collect the first two days. Monty got
another with Harrington in the Saturday afternoon fourballs; Langer, now in his mid-40s, having that session off.

The American team in 2002 was no push over. Tiger
Woods was now in his prime and only just a year past
his astonishing feat of winning all four major championships in succession, albeit not in one calendar
year. Payne Stewart may have gone, tragically killed in
an air crash just a month after the 1999 match, but had
been replaced by a fit Paul Azinger, fully recovered
from a brush with cancer – a player with one of the best
US records of those who had campaigned during the years
when Europe really was a force to be reckoned with.

Then there was Phil Mickelson, firmly established as
the second-best player in the world to Tiger Woods, and
who had won all three of his previous singles matches.
David Toms had by now won his major and was the
reigning US PGA Champion, and together with
Mickelson would win 2½ points together over the first
two days.

Woods, though, remained a problem for the United
States. In the two previous matches, at Valderrama and

Brookline, he had won just 2½ points out of a possible 8 in foursomes and fourballs. Things didn't get any better this time. The first morning he went out top with the rejuvenated Paul Azinger, yet Darren Clarke and Thomas Björn saw them off on the last green. This was a new European partnership, but one founded on great personal friendship, and with similar sorts of games – big and bold – just the right combination to stare down Woods that first morning.

Then in the afternoon Woods was sent out with another veteran Mark Calcavecchia, having his first game since that horrible collapse against Montgomerie at Kiawah Island in 1991. This would not have been the ideal way for Calcavecchia to come back into the Ryder Cup cauldron – all eyes always on Woods and all the extra pressure on just being his partner. They were duly beaten by the ebullient Westwood and Garcia, fresh off their first triumph that morning over David Duval and Davis Love. So now it was Woods 2½ points out of a possible 10!

Europe got off to a great start that first morning, with only Mickelson and Toms preventing a whitewash. In the afternoon it was some of the lesser lights of the US team that kept them in the game. Hal Sutton and Scott Verplank won the top foursome against Clarke and Björn, while Stewart Cink and Jim Furyk beat Padraig Harrington and Paul McGinley, an all-Ireland partnership that had won the World Cup in 1997, but never really came off in the Ryder Cup. They were good friends and had achieved much together, but did not have matching types of games, Harrington the archetypal scrambler, McGinley a neater, tidier player.

Throughout this great period for the Ryder Cup, Europe's success was founded in finding partnerships that worked and then getting the maximum out of them over those first two days. From the 1980s there was Faldo and Woosnam and Lyle and Langer; at The Belfry in 1985 there was Ballesteros and Manuel Pinero, and then the greatest of them all, Ballesteros and Olazábal. In the 1990s there was that one match where Faldo and Montgomerie did really well; then Clarke and Westwood plus Parnevik and Garcia performed heroics at Brookline. This time at The Belfry we had Garcia and Westwood and Langer and Montgomerie. The philosophy was always: you win, you keep going.

For a long time the Americans never seemed that bothered. Based on the years when they won all the time, their priority was to ensure every player got a game each day, regardless of how they were playing. Finding point-gathering partnerships never seemed that important to them and even to this day they have struggled to find any pairing that swept all before them. In this 2002 match at The Belfry, Mickelson and Toms came closest, but still only got 2½ points out of 4. Further evidence, perhaps, of the brotherhood spirit of the Europeans for these matches versus the more clinical isolationism of the Americans.

Certainly one of the winners that Friday afternoon, Sutton and Verplank never got another go together. Cink and Furyk were tried in the foursomes the following morning, but lost to Westwood and Garcia, and were then parted for the second series of fourballs, the format in which they had been successful the previous day. What did work for the Americans that Saturday was putting Davis Love with Tiger Woods.

Even so, the morning foursomes on day two were shared, once again Langer and Montgomerie, and Westwood and Garcia were the winners. For the Americans, Woods and Love were very good in disposing of Clarke and Björn out in the country. That series had always looked likely to be shared, with America's strong pairings at 1 and 4, Europe's at 2 and 3. Europe were still a point ahead at lunch.

For a long time that afternoon, it looked as though Europe would take a 2- or even 3-point lead into the singles. All the matches were close, and no sooner had Calcavecchia and Duval beaten Niclas Fasth and Parnevik at the 18th, than Monty and Harrington had levelled the series against America's best pair, Mickelson and Toms. Behind, Westwood and Garcia were always just in front of Woods and Love, and the final game – Clarke and McGinley against Hoch and Furyk – was all square.

Indeed, Westwood and Garcia were 1 up and two to play, and with only Garcia on the green in two at the par-5 17th, looked likely to win by 2/1. However, Garcia three-putted to lose that hole, and then Westwood did the same at 18, to present Woods and Love with a point they never looked like getting. Soon after that, Clarke and McGinley shook hands on the 18th green, having halved their match. All in all, a disappointing end to two days where Europe always seemed to hold the upper hand, but which in the end left the side all square, 8 points apiece, with the singles to come.

This was the first time since 1981 that, on home soil, Europe had not been ahead after the foursomes and fourballs, and this was still the era when the Americans were perceived as the more likely to win the final-day singles. Tony Jacklin's all-conquering team of 1985 had won the singles, and Bernard Gallacher had come from behind to win at Oak Hill ten years later, but singles had always seemed to be where the Americans were most comfortable. With all twelve players out on both sides, it was felt by most observers they had the strength in depth and, confirmed by the World Rankings, they were, man for man, just about the favourites.

Against that, a feeling had grown up that a lead going into the last day was something of a poisoned chalice. Time and again Europe had struggled to go on and win after our pairings and partnerships had enjoyed a great couple of days. Even in 1997, when Seve's side had been 5 ahead, the Sunday was a nerve-racking affair, and one that so nearly went wrong; then at Brookline, Europe had been 4 ahead going into the singles, but was on the slippery slope even before the US Team lost its head. And the one time the US had been ahead – that time at Oak Hill – they weren't able to close the deal. It is something to do with even a small lead putting that side on the defensive, while those behind can come out firing with nothing to lose.

And so, on the Saturday evening, there was disappointment that after such a good couple of days Europe had relatively little to show for it. For the long follower of these contests there was a certain relief that we weren't going to have another re-enactment of the old saga of defending some sort of lead throughout a desperately tense final day. And then, the draw for the singles came out.

One look and European hearts would have soared. There was our powerhouse all going out at the top of the draw, while Curtis Strange had kept most of his big guns to the end: 'The one thing I never changed was my singles order,' Torrance would later recall. 'Indeed, a year or two afterwards, I found in a drawer my original singles line-up for 2001, before it was postponed, and it was exactly the same as the one I sent out in the match itself.'

Many may have thought Torrance had taken a leaf out of Ben Crenshaw's book from 1999, when he put so much power at the top, but that hardly entered Torrance's head: 'Crenshaw had no option. He was 4 points behind and had to catch up quick. No, it was a member of Sunningdale, David "Bugsy" Holland – past captain of the club, and Harrovian Halford Hewitt player; a man of trenchant views and little time for the opinions of others – who categorically stated, "Put your best out first and the worst last".

'I thought about it long and hard and I couldn't think of a scenario where it wouldn't work. If we were ahead, I wanted them out there to finish the thing off; if we were behind I would want to catch up quickly. And I don't care who you are – Woods, Nicklaus – if you are playing in that bottom section, 8 to 12, you are fallible in this particular competition. You don't have to have your best at the end to cope, because as often as not, out of the shadows come heroes.'

The one thing Torrance cannot fail to have observed from Brookline was the effect on the crowd of the home nation's colour on the giant scoreboards. In 1999, it was the massive swathe of blue in the top matches that really got their crowd going, and created the unstoppable momentum that took them to victory. Three years later, Torrance did the same, as his powerhouse in the van painted the top of the boards red.

Colin Montgomerie was just about shaking hands, having beaten Scott Hoch 5/4, as Tiger Woods teed off in the last match against the out of form Jesper Parnevik. Indeed, Parnevik took much pleasure in pointing out how unlikely it was that their match was going to have any relevance in the outcome of the match; an observation that came true a few hours later, when, all square and one to play – and the Ryder Cup once again in Europe's grasp – they shook hands on the 18th fairway and called it a half. Woods' only revenge was to pinch Parnevik's nanny, Elin Nordegren, and make her his wife.

Not long after Monty had seen off Hoch, Langer, Harrington and Björn also posted wins. A clean sweep at the top was missed when Sergio Garcia frittered away an early lead against David Toms and Darren Clarke ground out a worthy half with David Duval. After that, though, it took a little time for the final nails to be put in the US coffin. Niclas Fasth was just ahead of Paul Azinger, McGinley was having a tremendous struggle with Jim Furyk, as were Pierre Fulke and Davis Love. Early on, it looked as though Phil Mickelson would overwhelm Philip Price, and no one was putting much money on Parnevik getting the better of Woods, even though the match was close.

Then, to echo Sam Torrance, out of the shadows came a hero. Phil Price was 3 down after just five holes, and with Mickelson right down the middle of the 6th fairway, Price almost drove into the lake on the left. Mickelson playing first hit his approach to some 4 feet: 4 up looked a certainty. But Price, almost standing in the water and the ball well above his feet, somehow hoiked it round, and up it scuttled just inside the American's ball. Mickelson missed, Price holed: 2 down, not 4. And what a turning point! Inspired, Price won one hole after another, until on the 16th he holed another long downhiller, Mickelson missed and Price had beaten the world's no. 2 by 3/2. The abiding cry of the celebrations that night was a Welsh voice calling out: 'Tell 'm who I beat; go on, tell 'm who I beat!'

That gave Europe 5½ points, while the US still only

had 1½, and there were still plenty of chances for the final point needed for victory. Niclas Fasth was 1 up and one to play against Paul Azinger, and comfortably on the green in two; Azinger in the bunker. But the American, showing all the guts for which he was renowned in the matches, holed for three and halved the match. Not bad for what would be your very last shot in the Ryder Cup! Fasth can feel poorly served by the bare statistics of the match; played three, lost two and just one halved point. But the two losses both came on the 18th green and in both he could be said to have been unlucky to lose. So, another half point was still required for Europe.

Next up it was another rookie, Paul McGinley, whose tally from the first two days was a loss and a half from two matches. He and Jim Furyk were all square coming up the last, and having witnessed Azinger's amazing escape from down the fairway, both knew the match was still alive. Both found the green, McGinley to putt first. He knocked it 8 feet by. Furyk missed, McGinley holed, and the celebrations began.

Had McGinley failed there was still another string to Europe's bow in that Pierre Fulke was also all square playing the last against Davis Love. But by now the scenes up at the 18th green were such that it would obviously be some time before they could play their seconds. With both on the fairway and the match now over, a look, a nod, and a handshake and another half-point was agreed. And with that it should be noted that all four rookies had gained at least a half, and each against a player who had won or would win a major championship. Very much a case of 'out of the shadows come heroes'.

Oakland Hills

14–19 September

Europe (*Bernard Langer*)	Matches		USA (*Hal Sutton*)
Fourballs: *Morning*			
C. Montgomerie & P. Harrington (2/1) 1		0	P. Mickelson & T. Woods
D. Clarke & M.A. Jiménez (5/4)	1	0	D. Love III & C. Campbell
P. McGinley & L. Donald (halved)	½	½	C. Riley & S. Cink (halved)
S. Garcia & L. Westwood (5/3)	1	0	D. Toms & J. Furyk
Foursomes: *Afternoon*			
M.A. Jiménez & T. Levet	0	1	C. DiMarco & J. Haas (3/2)
C. Montgomerie & P. Harrington (4/2)	1	0	D. Love III & F. Funk
D. Clarke & L. Westwood (1 hole)	1	0	P. Mickelson & T. Woods
S. Garcia & L. Donald (2/1)	1	0	K. Perry & S. Cink
Fourballs: *Morning*			
S. Garcia & L. Westwood (halved)	½	½	J. Haas & C. DiMarco (halved)
D. Clarke & I. Poulter	0	1	T. Woods & C. Riley (4/3)
P. Casey & D. Howell (1 hole)	1	0	J. Furyk & C. Campbell
C. Montgomerie & P. Harrington	0	1	S. Cink & D. Love III (3/2)
Foursomes: *Afternoon*			
D. Clarke & L. Westwood (5/4)	1	0	J. Haas & C. DiMarco
M.A. Jiménez & T. Levet	0	1	P. Mickelson & D. Toms (4/3)
S. Garcia & L. Donald (1 hole)	1	0	J. Furyk & F. Funk
P. Harrington & P. McGinley (4/3)	1	0	D. Love III & T. Woods
Singles			
P. Casey	0	1	T. Woods (3/2)
S. Garcia (3/2)	1	0	P. Mickelson
D. Clarke (halved)	½	½	D. Love III (halved)
D. Howell	0	1	J. Furyk (6/4)
L. Westwood (1 hole)	1	0	K. Perry
C. Montgomerie (1 hole)	1	0	D. Toms
L. Donald	0	1	C. Campbell (5/3)
M.A. Jiménez	0	1	C. DiMarco (1 hole)
T. Levet (1 hole)	1	0	F. Funk
I. Poulter (3/2)	1	0	C. Riley
P. Harrington (1 hole)	1	0	J. Haas
P. McGinley (3/2)	1	0	S. Cink
Europe	18½	9½	**USA**

CHAPTER ELEVEN

The Perfect Match

2004
Bernhard Langer

For the third match in a row the United States had opted for one of America's great old championship venues as the place to hold the 2004 Ryder Cup. Oakland Hills had played host to several US Opens, the most famous of which was Ben Hogan's win in 1951, and the most recent was Steve Jones's unlikely success in 1996. The PGA of America was enjoying being accepted by these hallowed courses now that the match excited so much interest and had become such a money-spinner for any course and its surrounding area.

In contrast to The Country Club five years earlier, Oakland Hills had plenty of space. For a start it had 36 holes, a whole separate course on which to house all the paraphernalia that goes with what had become the biggest golf event in the world. And it had much more room to accommodate the crowds of spectators, now regularly up to the 40,000 a day mark.

By going to these grand major Championship venues, the US still weren't making real use of home advantage. None of their players (nor indeed Europe's) had played at Oakland Hills since 1996, so apart from it being a classic example of American championship golf – all grass and trees – they didn't know it any better than Europe did. Contrast this to the European matches over the last 25 years: there have been four visits to The Belfry and one to Valderrama – all venues where we have regularly competed in the years leading up to the match. It would be the same in 2006 when the K Club outside Dublin was used. This had been the venue of the European Open for more than ten years.

This is mostly down to the European Tour now being in charge of staging the Ryder Cup. With their expertise in putting on big golf events they have taken over the running of it and even have a separate Ryder Cup division, whose sole job is to stage the event every four years and deal with the mass of ongoing detail in the intervening years. No sooner is one match finished, and in some respects even earlier, planning for the next gets underway. The year 2010 will see the Ryder Cup in Wales, and Ryder Cup Ltd has been working for several years making sure an awkward site will produce a successful event. The golf course has been greatly altered – several new holes added – just to make it work. This year the new course was used for the first time at the Celtic Manor Wales Open and a tournament will be played there each year up to the match. Any player will tell you, having the chance to compete over a course is much more beneficial than just having a knock round it in the days just prior to the match.

The European Tour and the PGA now maximise the commercial opportunities this massive event generates. Any country that wants to host the Ryder Cup – and Wales is no exception – has to guarantee not only one full-scale professional tournament each year leading up to the match, but a Challenge Tour event, a Seniors event and a ladies tournament; also a number of grass roots initiatives as well. The days when old die-hards were offended by the thought of the Ryder Cup repeatedly going back to The Belfry – once considered so unrepresentative of all that is best in British golf – are long gone.

In 2004, at Oakland Hills, Bernhard Langer was to be the captain. Deep passion had been at the root of so many of our recent successes – think of Jacklin, Seve and Torrance; some wondered how well Langer – never one to wear his heart on his sleeve – would blend his twelve charges into an efficient fighting machine. Certainly his style was different, but no less successful: 'What Bernhard brought to the job was extreme professionalism,' Colin Montgomerie remembers. 'There wasn't the passion of some of his predecessors, just magnificent efficiency. If I was to describe his style, I would call it ambassadorial. He was immaculate in everything he did, totally prepared; there was never a moment when you worried something might go wrong.

'By the way he conducted himself, lived his life, the way he had handled his career, won a couple of majors despite putting problems that would have broken a lesser man, Bernhard naturally had huge respect from the team. Whilst he was in charge, you felt that nothing had been left to chance, everything had been very carefully thought out.' And if Langer was the most organised, best prepared of European captains, he was up against someone – Hal Sutton – who seemed to be the exact opposite. Finally, Europe – probably for the very first time ever – had the better team.

It was certainly the first time devotees of the match felt Europe now had such strength in depth that any one of fifteen or eighteen players could have played their way into the side, and it would be none the weaker for it. Europe now had a bunch of competitive players, several of whom had benefited from the experience of going through the American college system – unquestionably the best nursery slopes for any aspiring tournament player. The likes of Luke Donald and Paul Casey had been to American colleges and come top of the class, and that, together with successful Walker Cup careers, meant that no American held any fear for them.

The major champions Tony Jacklin had been able to rely on were now gone, but there was an equally strong nucleus to the team. Clarke, Westwood, Garcia, Montgomerie and Harrington were all seasoned Ryder Cup campaigners, all with more wins than losses under their belt. They genuinely enjoyed the pressures of this particular competition. Casey and Donald, with their American achievements – and already with victories around Europe and elsewhere to their credit – were a great promise both for this match and the future. Most important, the gap – if indeed there was one between the top few and the rest – was negligible. In 2004 Langer captained a side that batted all the way down.

The selection process for the European team had changed again. With quite a number of our players now competing as much in America as Europe, it was decreed that half the automatic places would be decided by world ranking points and half by order of merit position on the European Tour, the captain retaining the right to pick the last two. It was not an easy selection system to follow because the European Ryder Cup world ranking points list operated only from the September before the match and was different to the official world ranking issued on a weekly basis that reflected individual performances over a three year period. Confused? Many of us were.

Compared with some of his predecessors, Langer had a relatively easy task in choosing his two wildcards. Luke Donald has always played predominantly in America and by 2004 had already won the Southern Farm Bureau Classic over there. With its total fixation on length and putting ability, the American Tour is difficult for good all-rounders to shine on, and while Donald was making a comfy living there, he wasn't making his mark in the world ranking section. With his superb amateur career – and more than competent professional one – he was an obvious candidate for Langer's team, but would have to prove himself in Europe if he was genuinely interested in making the side. After the 2004 Open Championship at Troon, he stayed on, played a few events, won one and finished third in another. Case proven! He also won in Switzerland immediately after selection, as if to underwrite Langer's faith in him.

This was now going to be a team with five rookies in it. Unlike Mark James, Langer had a high regard for experience and at that point was missing the most experienced player of the lot, Colin Montgomerie. Monty had won at the beginning of the year, but had not had a good summer, and was not in the team as of right. Golf tournaments are hard enough to win under normal circumstances: add the pressures of trying to make the team and they become fiendish. The harder Monty tried, the worse he played. But there was the glimmer of old routines returning in the couple of weeks leading up to the team announcement and when Monty's name was added to that of Donald, no one questioned Langer's selections.

Langer was also mindful that, as he had played relatively little in Europe, he didn't know the younger element of his side that well. Wisely, having already chosen Anders Forsbrand as his principle aide – a good friend but someone who had never played in the Ryder Cup – he waited to see which of the senior European players didn't make the side and added Thomas Björn to his management team. It was an early example of a shrewdness that would mark his entire campaign.

Langer had played under four different captains – Jacklin, Seve, Gallacher and Torrance: 'They all did a great job and all did it slightly differently', he later said. 'I tried to pick out all that I thought positive from what they did and incorporate it in my captaincy. I definitely learned that you want to play every player before Sunday. You don't want to have anybody sitting out all week and throw them in the deep end without having played before. That was a bit of a dilemma as I had such a strong team and so many strong pairings, but I had to break them up to get the other guys in.

'Then I sent little cards to each player asking them to give me one or two names of players they would prefer to play with and one or two you would not want to. All their answers were confidential, but they were a great help in getting me to think only of pairings that would be acceptable to all concerned, not waste my time considering partnerships that wouldn't have worked anyway.' Then, with a twinkle in his eye and a little smile, he added, 'That way I don't think I would ever have ended up putting Tiger Woods and Phil Mickelson together.'

'I did a few other things; I researched colours, what they mean to us as human beings. It is a proven fact that some colours are more aggressive than other colours and some colours you feel better in than others. Little things like that; some of them had been done before and I copied them, and I brought one or two new things of my own.

'I think personal conversations are very important, more so almost than team meetings. I talked individually to all the guys most days. It was particularly important to speak to all those who were not going to be playing in one of the foursomes or fourballs; important to reassure them it was not anything to do with them not playing well. In the stress of that competition it is important to keep reminding them that you still think they are great players, wouldn't be there if they weren't, but that, with four having to sit out each series the first two days, they just couldn't be part of it that time.'

While Langer was quietly honing his highly talented squad, his opposite number, Hal Sutton, was single-handedly writing a manual on how not to captain a Ryder Cup team. His pairings were an almost open book, the Woods/Mickelson partnership having been a matter of public debate for some weeks. Even the American press queried the wisdom of it. There was a well-known antipathy between them and the sense that, even if they did win their matches, where was the fun, the excitement and the glory? They were nos. 1 and 2 in the world, and so were expected to win. Also, they hardly practiced together. Mickelson had followed his habit of researching the course some weeks before the contest and spending the days immediately prior to it practicing elsewhere. Sutton allowed this, as he was following the Jack Nicklaus ethos of captaincy by telling his team to prepare for the Ryder Cup like any other event and follow their usual routines. Woods and Mickelson certainly didn't play any foursomes together in practice and there can have been little discussion about whose make of ball would be played. Woods drove the odds, so it was his Nike ball that they played that afternoon, and the first time Mickelson had used a Nike ball in competition was when he hit the second shot to the opening hole off Woods' drive.

Mickelson also had a new set of clubs in his bag. In recent years his philosophy has been to play serious competitive golf the first eight months of the year and recharge the batteries between September and Christmas. He believes this to be the best way to look after his physical and mental attributes and make his playing career as long as possible. Should he be contemplating a change of clubs – and he was in 2004 – he will make that change immediately after his season has finished, and so give himself the maximum time to get comfortable with the new set. While that might have been good for Mickelson in the 2005 golf season, it didn't say much for his commitment to the US cause in the Ryder Cup.

Elsewhere, the US side had a slightly strange look to it. Kenny Perry, having been little more than a good journeyman for the best part of twenty years, suddenly flowered in midsummer 2003. He won three tournaments out of the four he played either side of the US Open and, with the US two-year qualifying period, there and then played his way into the team. His only other achievement had been to tie for the 1996 US PGA Championship at Valhalla, only to lose the play-off to

Mark Brookes. By 2004 he had returned to his more mundane level and by the Ryder Cup wasn't playing well at all.

Then there was Chris Riley. From nowhere he suddenly appeared in the side in the final week of qualifying. The last thing he would have been thinking about when he teed it up in the US PGA Championship at Whistling Straits was making the US Ryder Cup team. But a fourth place there, just a shot outside joining V.J. Singh, Justin Leonard and Chris DiMarco in a play-off and he was in the team. He was a man of slender build who didn't hit the ball far, but was nevertheless a brilliant putter. He would form an unlikely but successful partnership with Tiger Woods on the second day.

Finally, there was Jay Haas, playing only his second Ryder Cup match, and 21 years after his first. His golf had been rejuvenated by the growing excellence of his son Billy, who had played in the Walker Cup the year before and Haas Snr was himself just embarking on the Champions Tour. Amazing how, being competitive once again among your peers sharpens up your skills. He didn't quite make the team as of right, but with a lack of obvious talent elsewhere, Sutton gave him one of his two berths. After all, they were contemporaries.

Knowing that Sutton was going to put Mickelson and Woods together and send them out top, Langer chose Montgomerie and Harrington to go up against them. They had played a game together at The Belfry in 2002 and combined in a fourball to beat Mickelson and David Toms, who were America's most successful pairing that year. It was fourballs that first morning at Oakland Hills and with Montgomerie birdying the first hole, he and Harrington played the first six holes in five under par. That gave them a lead they would never relinquish. Sutton's great scheme had been holed below the waterline.

That win was of great significance to Montgomerie. In the time since his selection, his golf hadn't noticeably improved and he arrived in America more than a little concerned. His legendary accuracy off the tee and through the green was missing. In his playing days Langer was never known for giving his fellow competitors helpful advice. Nothing malicious, but they were all after the same pot, so where's the sense in helping them? One of the idiosyncrasies of Monty's swing is that he always starts with his hands leading the club away, head and shaft only catching up as the swing progresses. Langer noticed this had become too pronounced, suggested a bit of tightening up and suddenly the metronomic repetitiveness was back. Montgomerie's play in that most important top match confirmed he was back in the groove.

The first morning proved most satisfactory. Behind Monty and Harrington there were a couple of thumping victories – Darren Clarke and Miguel Angel Jiménez beating Davis Love and Chad Campbell 5/4, and Sergio Garcia and Lee Westwood – a partnership that Sam Torrance had stumbled on almost by accident two years previously – again came good, beating the formidable-on-paper combination of David Toms and Jim Furyk by 5/3. Only Luke Donald and Paul McGinley failed to make it a clean sweep by only getting a half. 'Only' a half! In years gone by there were times when halves were like gold dust!

It was now you began to see the intricate dance of Langer's plans. He knew that for the first time a European captain had a twelve-man team all of whom were more than capable of doing themselves and

Europe proud. There were no passengers. His avowed intent was to play everyone before the singles and with the talent at his disposal he could afford to start bringing in early those who hadn't played in the morning. He also shuffled some of his successful pairings.

Monty and Harrington stayed together because they were as good at foursomes as fourballs, but Garcia was paired with Donald and Westwood was back with his old chum Clarke. Westwood and Clarke had the pleasure of handing a second defeat to Woods and Mickelson, so putting a final nail in the coffin of that partnership and heaping humiliation on its creator, Hal Sutton.

If Woods and Mickelson couldn't succeed at fourballs, they were unlikely to find a winning blend in the delicate art of foursomes. They played competently enough and were still in with a chance standing on the 18th tee. It was Mickelson to drive and with a 3-wood for safety hit it so far wide, 80 yards off line and nearly out of bounds. Simon Barnes of The Times – a beautiful writer but no fan of golf – was watching and summed up Woods' reaction: 'The best moment of the tournament', he later wrote in his book The Meaning of Sport, 'was the look on Woods' face when Phil Mickelson hit that drive. It was an expression of bemused contempt, mixed with the thought: what the f*** am I doing here?'

The only European partnership that didn't work that afternoon – nor would it the following day – was the Continental pairing of Jiménez and Thomas Levet. Sutton, meanwhile, continued with that old American habit of giving everyone a game on the first day, regardless of how they were playing. Maybe though, having had so little success in the morning, he felt his only chance was wholesale change. The only change he didn't make was the one he should have done, which was to split Woods and Mickelson before their disintegration did team morale more damage. Europe 6½, the USA 1½ was the magical scoreline at the end of day one.

Fourballs again on Saturday morning meant it was time to give the remaining players who hadn't played yet an outing. Ian Poulter came in to partner Darren Clarke, while Paul Casey and David Howell – neither of whom had played that well in practice – were to get their one chance. For a time it looked as though the morning was going to go horribly wrong. Clarke and Poulter never got into their stride and the banker pairing, Montgomerie and Harrington also had an off day.

Garcia and Westwood had a tremendous tussle at the top and squeaked a half, but that looked as though it might be all with Casey and Howell 1 down and two to play against Jim Furyk and Chad Campbell. But Howell got a two at 17 to square and then they won the 18th as well. It may only have been a single point, but from a psychological perspective it was enormous. On a morning that could so easily gone 4–nil to the United States, 2½–1½ almost seemed like a win.

One of the big US wins that morning came from the unlikely pairing of Woods and Chris Riley. Woods seemed to relish his role of senior partner, shepherding the new boy round. Riley had shown his mettle getting the single half-point America managed the first morning with Stewart Cink, and now dovetailed well with Woods to beat Clarke and Poulter. Here, surely, was a partnership made for foursomes, with Riley short but accurate and Woods with plenty of everything to fill in any gaps.

Unbelievably, Riley told Sutton he didn't want to play in the afternoon, as he didn't really understand foursomes and Sutton accepted it! The real culprit though was Woods. He had clearly had a most enjoyable morning, lots of smiles and chats – as you do when you are winning – but never came down from his private Mount Olympus and cajoled, demanded even, that he and Riley should go out again. He was the one who should have taken the lead, but maybe, after the dreadful day his captain had condemned him to with Mickelson, he wasn't in the mood.

The other winning US partnership that second morning was Cink and Love against Monty and Harrington, yet they too were split up for the afternoon. Cink was left on the sidelines, while Love was put with Woods and they were soundly beaten by Ireland in the form of Harrington and Paul McGinley. No wonder the word was going round that the best European captain after Bernhard Langer was Hal Sutton!

So it was back to the old routine in the afternoon, with three of the same partnerships that had played so well in foursomes the previous day going out again. The only change was that Monty got the afternoon off – the first time since his inaugural match in 1991 he had missed playing in every series; what a record! He was now in his 40s, and he knew as well as anyone the stresses and strains of these contests. He had earned an afternoon off.

The scoreline was much the same too. Three games went Europe's way, two by big margins. The one close one – Donald and Garcia against Jim Furyk and Fred Funk – might easily have gone America's way, but the US were finding out what we had known for years: that holing putts and winning matches when you desperately need to are very difficult to come by. With just the singles to come, the score – unbelievable as it may seem

– was Europe 11, the United States 5. We had arrived with high hopes, but this was the stuff of dreams.

The task now was to complete the job, not just win the match, but win the singles as well: 'I told the guys not to go in there with the mentality that we are six points ahead,' Langer remembers. 'Look at this like it is a fresh start, a fresh match. We had won three out of the four series of fourballs and foursomes, now let's win the singles too. Go in there like we are level and beat them at this as well.'

The Americans had a mountain to climb. To win the match they needed to win nine of the twelve games and halve another. The only way to do that, as Crenshaw had so ably shown five years before (and Torrance to a lesser extent in 2002) was to get your colour on the board at the start; to get ahead in several matches, apply some pressure, and just maybe undermine the confidence of opposition coming behind. Bereft of sub-tlety, Sutton just banged out his twelve in world ranking order, Woods at the top. Langer could almost have writ-ten down their order without seeing it.

Paul Casey was the one chosen to take on the world no. 1. He's a tough nut with great self-belief. At his best he can beat anyone, as he would show a couple of years on in the World Match Play at Wentworth. He hadn't been playing well coming into the match, but had had that great win with David Howell on the Saturday morn-ing and that might just be the spark he needed. He was also fresh, having only played the one game.

Langer too put much of his power near the top, had Jiménez and Levet near the end – they had not really got their games together that week – and then had Harrington and McGinley in the last two games. These two good friends specifically asked to be in adjoining matches, as there was a considerable Irish contingent out for the Ryder Cup and if they were next to one another then this phalanx of support would not be divided.

America did get the start they were desperate for. Within the hour they were up in the top five matches. It was Garcia that first cracked the blue wall being built on the scoreboard. Two down after three holes to Mickelson, with neither playing elegant golf, he somehow contrived good figures from impossible places and was ahead by the turn. He might just have been a young Seve in his prime. He pulled ahead coming home to win by 3/2 – a victory worth far more than the 1 point it put on the board.

Others then began to get into their stride. Darren Clarke brought Davis Love back to all square and that was the way it would end. With Westwood just getting the better of Kenny Perry, it was now a question of who would hole the winning putt and where it would happen. It was to be the stuff of fairy tales.

Luke Donald had run into some brilliant figures from Chad Campbell and lost out in the country, and the other games behind were pretty close and had some way to go. Up the 18th came Colin Montgomerie, 1 up on David Toms. A win for Monty and another Ryder Cup victory would have been achieved. Both were on the green in two, Toms closer to the hole. Monty putted first, to 6 feet, Toms again inside, but not dead. Montgomerie straight in the middle and the job was done. May the celebrations begin!

It was the 18th green, it was the putt that won the Ryder Cup and it was Colin Montgomerie who holed it. For so long he had been at the heart of Europe's efforts in this biennial contest, for so long the rock on which so many hard and close-fought victories had been forged. It was only right that once again his was the game that determined where the Ryder Cup would spend the next two years.

Europe was able to celebrate that afternoon on and around the 18th green, and no one could be offended. It would be twenty minutes before another game hove into sight and by then order had been restored. Poulter and McGinley had wrapped up their matches on the 16th green, Levet and Harrington came up the last and they too both won. Langer's final wish had been achieved: the singles had been comprehensively won as well. The final result? 18½–9½ .

Obviously, Bernhard Langer could have gone on to have another go at home, at the K Club in 2006, but by now those great players from the 1980s were coming to their time. Of all those players Langer was still the most serious competitor. He still had playing rights both in America and Europe and would come awfully close to winning again on the US Tour. The Champions Tour was just three years away and when he turned fifty he planned to plunder that as well. No, he had done his job and won his match, and as all who know him would have expected, he had done it perfectly.

CHAPTER TWELVE

The Icing on the Cake

2006
Ian Woosnam

The Ryder Cup in Ireland was almost a celebration of the previous 25 years, during which time the contest had been transformed from a depressingly one-sided, biennial symphony of defeat to a number of glorious victories – often against the most challenging of odds. Ireland had been starved of great international sporting events for too long and the arrival of the Ryder Cup in 2006 was anticipated for months, even years, before it actually arrived. A Ryder Cup usually involves the participation of a town, a city, a county or a state, but by the time it came to Ireland the whole nation wanted a part of it. The whole nation wanted to be there.

And it was a wonderful opportunity for Ireland to show off its wares. Some weeks after the event the *Spectator* magazine – not a vehicle known for dabbling too much in things sporting – described it as, 'the

K Club

22-24 September

Europe (*Ian Woosnam*)	Matches		USA (*Tom Lehman*)

Fourballs: *Morning*

C. Montgomerie & P. Harrington	0	1	T. Woods & J. Furyk (1 hole)
P. Casey & R. Karlsson (halved)	½	½	S. Cink & J.J. Henry (halved)
S. Garcia & J.M. Olazábal (3/2)	1	0	D. Toms & B. Wetterich
D. Clarke & L. Westwood (1 hole)	1	0	P. Mickelson & C. DiMarco

Foursomes: *Afternoon*

P. McGinley & P. Harrington (halved)	½	½	C. Campbell & Z. Johnson (halved)
D. Howell & H. Stenson (halved)	½	½	S. Cink & D. Toms (halved)
L. Westwood & C. Montgomerie (halved)	½	½	P. Mickelson & C. DiMarco (halved)
L. Donald & S. Garcia (2 holes)	1	0	T. Woods & J. Furyk

Fourballs: *Morning*

P. Casey & R. Karlsson (halved)	½	½	S. Cink & J.J. Henry
S. Garcia & J.M. Olazábal (3/2)	1	0	P. Mickelson & C. DiMarco
L. Westwood & D. Clarke (3/2)	1	0	T. Woods & J. Furyk
H. Stenson & P. Harrington	0	1	Z. Johnson & S. Verplank (2/1)

Foursomes: *Afternoon*

S. Garcia & L. Donald (2/1)	1	0	P. Mickelson & D. Toms
C. Montgomerie & L. Westwood (halved)	½	½	C. Campbell & V. Taylor (halved)
P. Casey & D. Howell (5/4)	1	0	S. Cink & Z. Johnson
P. Harrington & P. McGinley	0	1	T. Woods & J. Furyk (3/2)

Singles

C. Montgomerie (1 hole)	1	0	D. Toms
S. Garcia	0	1	S. Cink (4/3)
P. Casey (2/1)	1	0	J. Furyk
R. Karlsson	0	1	T. Woods (3/2)
L. Donald (2/1)	1	9	C. Campbell
P. McGinley (halved)	½	½	J.J. Henry (halved)
D. Clarke (3/2)	1	0	Z. Johnson
H. Stenson (4/3)	1	0	V. Taylor
D. Howell (5/4)	1	0	B. Wetterich
J.M. Olazábal (2/1)	1	0	P. Mickelson
L. Westwood (2 holes)	1	0	C. DiMarco
P. Harrington	0	1	S. Verplank (4/3)

Europe	18½	9½	**USA**

biggest, most meticulously planned, strategically executed, state of the art advertisement in the world – for Ireland'. It was a meeting of the organisational skills of the European Tour, by now well versed at putting on this massive event in diverse locations around Europe every four years, and the Irish Tourist Board, Failte Ireland: 'The eyes of the world are on County Kildare,' Paul Keeley of Failte Ireland said at the time. 'With the Ryder Cup, you have an opportunity to sell your country', and Ireland certainly made the most of it.

It would have been lovely had the match been able to grace one of Ireland's great links courses, most probably Portmarnock. For many years the Irish Open had been played there and attracted crowds barely smaller than those that made the pilgrimage to The Open Championship, also played exclusively at the seaside. But the Ryder Cup is now big business and to win the right to stage it requires considerable financial resources. In Ireland's case those resources were to be found in the Smurfit Packaging Co., and, specifically, Dr Michael Smurfit, its Chairman and CEO. And he had his own train set. It was called the K Club.

Twenty or so years previously, Dr Michael had acquired Straffen House, a handsome Georgian mansion set in rolling parkland some 20 miles south-west of Dublin. He immediately started building a golf course in the grounds, of sufficient stature to reflect the grandeur of the house. He commissioned Arnold Palmer to design it. The course opened in 1991 and in 1995 it became the home of the European Open. Dr Michael then started a campaign to bring the Ryder Cup to Ireland, beat off the opposition – no mean feat nowadays – and earned the right for 2006. To fund a Ryder Cup is a big commitment over several years and while Smurfit continued to sponsor the European Open, Borde Failte, a tremendous promoter of golf in Ireland, ensured other elements of the contract were fulfilled.

To start with, the Palmer Course was a bit of an ugly duckling – most new courses are until they mature and the trees grow in. Nestling alongside a tributary of the Liffy, it initially had a problem or two of flooding during bad weather, and with the Ryder Cup being in September, bad weather was a distinct possibility. As had been the case with Jaime Ortiz-Patino and Valderrama, Dr Michael had the resources and the expertise to sort any problems out. By the time the Ryder Cup came along the K Club was ready.

Bernhard Langer had decided one match was enough. The rest of that great crop of players (after Seve and himself), Nick Faldo, Ian Woosnam and Sandy Lyle, were now at the end of the days when they could compete seriously on the main tours, and a year or two short of being ready for the Champions Tour, the current name for the seniors' playground in the US. They were lining up for the job. If they were to take on the captaincy, now was the time. In the old days, captaincy – of anything – was seen as honour to be bestowed, not a job to be applied for. That didn't stop Woosnam and Faldo 'throwing their cap into the ring', almost simultaneously and to hell with the niceties of waiting to be asked.

Many had thought Woosnam would be the man to lead the side in Wales in 2010. The feisty Welshman felt sooner rather than later would be best; by 2010 he would be 52 and if he was going to compete successfully on the Champions Tour, would, by then, be fully committed over there. Everyone expected that Faldo would do the job sometime, but weren't sure exactly when that would be. It didn't take the Ryder Cup committee long to pencil Woosnam in for 2006 and Faldo two years later in America, where he was now based, working full-time for CBS as a commentator.

By now the captain's job was very different from the days of Tony Jacklin. Where he had to chase around and make certain every little detail was right for his team, there is now a whole department, a secretariat if you like, to look after all the housekeeping elements – the flights, the accommodation, the team uniforms, all the food and drink and transport, are all now taken care of. The Ryder Cup has become such a money-spinner, such an enormous business with a turnover measured in millions, there is now someone else to look after all such matters: the captain only has to concentrate on the players in his team.

And what a team was emerging for 2006! The two-tiered system of half from current world ranking points and half from the European order of merit was catching just about everyone in its net. Of the team that won so well at Oakland Hills, only Thomas Levet and Miguel Angel Jiménez were below the radar and two very strong Scandinavians had played their way in to replace them.

Robert Karlsson had been unlucky to miss out in Mark James's side of 1999; he had been 11th in the Order of Merit standings, but didn't catch the captain's eye when the wildcards were handed out. He then went into something of a decline and although he won a couple of tournaments in 2001 and 2002, had spent long periods in the doldrums. He knew how to win when he got the chance, but consistency was the problem, that and a tendency to be overcritical of his own shortcomings. By 2005 he had remodelled his swing and burst back on the scene the following summer, winning at the venue, but not the course, where the Ryder Cup would be played in 2010, Celtic Manor. Just about the tallest player in tournament golf at 6 feet 5 inches, his vast frame always looked too big to fit a swing into. When he appeared that summer it was with a new compact and repeating swing. Later he added the Deutsche Bank TPC of Europe to his collection and was not going to have to rely on his captain's goodwill this time to make the side.

Henrik Stenson was just 25 when he won The Benson and Hedges in 2001, but soon after his driving totally deserted him; he just hit it all over the place. For two years he struggled under the eye of coach Pete Cowan and slowly it came back. He won at Woburn in the autumn of 2004 and the following year had a number of high finishes to move into the top ten of the European rankings: a position he hasn't been out of since. He, too, booked his place in Woosnam's side early. The rest making automatic selection were all proven Ryder Cup campaigners and all had been part of those successful teams of recent times.

Not in the team as of right were Darren Clarke and Lee Westwood. Clarke, of course, had had to live the previous few years with his wife Heather's seemingly endless battle with cancer. It was a battle she would finally lose that summer and it was generally assumed the Ryder Cup would come too soon for him to want to take part. He'd played few events that year and was nowhere near making the team, but Woosnam would always have wanted such a potent force were he to be available. With sufficient time between the funeral and the match, Darren saw the positives of going to Ireland

for the match rather than grieving at home. A successful few days at the K Club could be the best therapy of
all.

His great friend Lee Westwood had taken a long
break after the match in 2004 during which his wife had
delivered their second child. Lee took a bit of a sabbat-
ical to enjoy the moment. When he returned, the sharp-
ness of his game had disappeared. A year and a half
later it still hadn't fully returned, and he, too, hadn't
done enough to be in the team as of right.

Had Clarke declared himself unavailable, Woosnam's
task would have been easy. Of those not already in the
team, Westwood and Thomas Björn stood out. They
would have been his choices. Now, though, it was a case
of which two from the eligible three, and Woosnam
experienced the first difficult moment of his captaincy.
He was not the first to find, in all the hullabaloo of
decision time, he couldn't have all the conversations
with the players concerned he should have had prior to
the announcement.

On that year's form alone it shouldn't have been a
contest. Thomas Björn was just outside the top dozen,
had already won the Irish Open back in May, and was
having a much better year than Westwood. But with
Clarke declaring himself a runner, and with all the
emotional pressures he would be under, Woosnam
realised how important it would be for Clarke to have
his great chum alongside him. Picking Westwood over
Björn was not an easy decision – Björn was a very good
friend of Clarke's too. It wasn't the obvious decision,
but it was the one he took. His only mistake was not to
tell Björn about it before the team was announced.

Björn had been in Germany for the BMW Open and
was still there; indeed, had hung on hoping to hear

from Woosnam one way or other, expecting good news in view of his relatively good year and superior position in the rankings. Whatever the reason, and possibly because he was trying to get hold of Westwood who was already on his way home and in the air, Woosnam failed to tell Björn the bad news. It was lack of courtesy, but whether he deserved the volley of abuse meted out in the press the following day is open to doubt. If harsh things are to be said, it is best they don't get said through the press. It was an inauspicious start to Woosnam's campaign.

That, though, was just about all that did go wrong. Woosnam, like Langer before him, had the problem, not of where to find the pairings to take on and beat the United States, but of how to keep his team of all stars happy when four out of the twelve had to sit out each of the four series of fourballs and foursomes. Just three players – Westwood, Harrington and Garcia – would play in every series: what a difference from the days of Tony Jacklin, when half the side – and sometimes more – would play every time out of sheer necessity. It was, indeed, an embarrassment of riches.

And what a luxury to be able to go into the first set of fourballs with players ranked ten, twelve and thirteen in the world sitting out! Again, most of the pairings had a familiar look to them: Harrington and Montgomerie, Garcia and Olazábal, and Clarke and Westwood. If Woosnam's intuition had been correct to put Westwood in the team to be there for Darren Clarke, it was also spot on to play them together in the fourballs. Without the emotional turmoil in Clarke's life, this was a partnership that might by now have run its course, but under the circumstances it was right to play them together again. The first morning they won a close encounter against Phil Mickelson and Chris DiMarco.

The importance of a win over those two cannot be exaggerated. In recent times the US have had difficulty in finding partnerships that work, that can build up a track record – especially with their elite players, Woods and Mickelson. However, in the previous year's Presidents Cup – the match between the USA and the rest of the World without Europe and played in the intervening years between Ryder Cups – two good partnerships had emerged: Mickelson and DiMarco, and Tiger Woods with Jim Furyk. It was important to curtail these budding relationships as quickly as possible.

The year 2006 was Woods's fifth Ryder Cup and yet no enduring partner has been found for him. Indeed, his overall record of twelve losses in twenty matches played in foursomes and fourballs is modest by any standards. One of the mysteries of golf is – as Simon Barnes observes in his book, *The Meaning of Sport* – why is it, 'that Colin Montgomerie is well-nigh unbeatable when playing for a team, yet beset by saucy doubts when on his own or in a major tournament; and why Tiger Woods is utterly dominant when he plays stroke play golf, but when part of a team he sulks in his cell.'

It is amazing that no American captain has yet done with Woods what Jacklin did with Seve all those years ago: take him aside, make him his hero – captain on the pitch if you like – ask him to find a player with whom he would like to take on this one form of the game that he has so far failed to excel in, and launch him on his way. Yes, it is pandering to his ego, and teams supposedly don't work if egos are on the loose, but Woods losing more often than not in the Ryder Cup is far more damaging to team morale than a bit of elitism. If he can't win, how on earth can the rest of them?

Woods got off to a winning start that first morning, despite hitting his opening shot into the lake on the left. Part of Woosnam's preparation for this campaign was to have some 100 new trees strategically planted – several were up the right-hand side of this opening hole – just to tighten up the course. What satisfaction to have claimed such a notable scalp so early!

That top point, won by Woods and Furyk against Harrington and Montgomerie, was the only one the US did win the first morning. They got a half in the second match, Stewart Cink and J.J. Henry sharing the honours with Casey and Karlsson. Garcia and Olazábal continued the enhancement of Garcia's blossoming record in the Ryder Cup and most satisfying of all, especially for Woosnam, was that win for Clarke and Westwood against Mickelson and DiMarco.

That was one of America's hotpot pairings nipped in the bud and in three goes together they would gather just a single half-point. Most unfairly, when they were finally parted, it was DiMarco who was dropped after being by far the better of the two over those first three games. Mickelson went out on the Saturday afternoon with his old partner David Toms, but they, too, lost to that successful foursomes pairing from Oakland Hills, Garcia and Luke Donald. By the time the next match comes round, their record in foursomes will be played four, won four.

These were cold wet days – as Ireland can so often produce in mid-September. But the natives had waited many a year for this one and rain or no, they were going to be there. The roars and cheers rang out even though this was not the weather, nor the course, for sparkling golf. Results had to be ground out, worked for, patiently waited for. It was a contest to get ahead in, and stay there, as morale was hard to keep up if things weren't going your way.

That first afternoon was the hardest graft of all. All four games went to the final hole and time and again Europe denied the visitors any crumb of comfort. Three of the games ended all square, the last another win for Garcia and Donald, and most satisfyingly it was against Woods and Furyk. Both series that first day had gone to Europe by 2½–1½.

Saturday morning saw Europe begin to draw away. They had two handsome wins and both against pairings that contained Woods and Mickelson. Psychologically, when you beat Woods in this contest, it feels like two points taken from the Americans, and the reverse is true for them: their icon loses, what chance have they got? Having dealt with Mickelson and Toms on the first day, Clarke and Westwood now took on and beat Woods and Furyk. How good that must have felt for Woosnam, the justification of his team selection. And what a job Westwood was doing, playing great golf and providing all the right support for his grieving mate both on and off the course.

Woosnam's deft touch was further demonstrated by only playing Clarke once each day, and in fourballs at that. Much emotion would have been spent in the days and weeks leading up to the match, he would not have had his usual bottomless well of energy, and adrenaline and five games would be too much. He was also going through major adjustments to his swing with Ewen Murray of Sky Sports, himself a tournament professional from earlier days, and with a keen eye and obvious communication skills.

For all his life, Darren had been a drawer of the ball and, blessed with enormous natural talent, had spent his early years trying to keep out of his own way, to let his raw skills produce the results. Often they did: there were those wins in World Golf Championships, the matchplay in 2000 and the NEC in 2003. But they were not enough and that one shape shot meant that too often there were pin positions on right-hand sides of greens he could not get at. In 2006 he was working on a fade, as and when it was required, and having to concentrate so heavily on his swing during this difficult year was perhaps the best way of keeping the demons off the course at bay. Foursomes in the Ryder Cup might, at this early stage, have been too stiff an examination.

It was another 2½ points to Europe that Saturday morning and the only cloud on the Irish horizon was that their own Padraig Harrington and Paul McGinley were not having a good time. McGinley had had to work hard just to make the team – a year's effort that had drained him and would leave little in the tank for 2007. He didn't seem to have much remaining at the K Club either and the pair of them only gleaned a disappointing half-point from two sets of foursomes. With the evidence from several World Cup outings, where foursomes had been their downfall, putting them together in that discipline might have been one of Woosnam's few errors.

The final afternoon of foursomes produced yet another 2½ points for Europe and while they weren't as far ahead going into the singles as they had been on other occasions, they had, for the first time, won each of the four series. A win in the singles would bring yet another record and 4 points ahead with 12 to go was handsome enough. Confidence was high, as for the first time ever our world ranking stature through the team was higher than that of the Americans'. We had won the Ryder Cup when logic and statistics said we shouldn't; surely we could bring it home when, on paper, we were the better side?

Montgomerie was given pole position that Sunday morning. His opponent was past US PGA Champion David Toms, now not quite the force of a year or two previously, and someone who had always been a bit short on self-belief. Monty liked to play quickly and if he performed as usual, he would soon have a splash of red up there to encourage those coming behind. This he did, but was never that far in front and in the end had to go to the 18th before claiming the match. It hadn't been a great week by his standards, but that point in a match the Americans thought they had a chance to win was an important blow.

Before long it was apparent there would be no miracle comeback for America. They'd never had to rely on great comebacks in their glory years and as these matches had got ever more competitive, they'd yet to acquire the skill; also, losing is a habit that can be hard to shake off. There were a few bright and brave spots: Stewart Cink produced some unbelievable figures to leave Garcia with a rare singles defeat, and Woods was more than competent in dealing with Karlsson – but that was about it.

A raft of big leads was being built in the middle and from somewhere in there the winning putt would emerge. For a moment it looked like we might have the perfect ending as Darren Clarke was about to close out his match on the 16th. First, though, Henrik Stenson beat Vaughn Taylor on the 15th to ensure Europe could not lose, then almost simultaneously Luke Donald finished his game against Chad Campbell to clinch the victory. Somehow it didn't matter. As Clarke made it three wins out of three for his personal tally, the tears and the champagne flowed. It had been Europe 18½, USA 9½ at Oakland Hills and it was the same here at home.

It is questionable whether Ian Woosnam enjoyed his stint of captaincy as much as those who had done it before, in particular Bernhard Langer, who had won – over there – by the same margin. Woosnam got off on the wrong foot with Thomas Björn over the question of his wildcard selections and seemed on the defensive with the press throughout. The stresses and strains of asking young, fit, world-class players to sit out this series or that is almost as stressful as telling someone he isn't going to get a wildcard selection – far more difficult than trying to squeeze an unlikely win from an inferior squad. Not long after the match was over, Woosnam was struck down with Chronic Fatigue Syndrome, which took more than a year to shake off. Whether it was the stress of the job, who knows, but captaincy – even of a winning squad – is now a huge commitment: lovely to have done, especially a winning one, but it does take a toll.

Whatever the future of these matches, this surely was the high watermark of Europe's endeavour. It had been a long road from all those perennial losses in the early years. It had required great vision, much effort and enormous skill and courage first to make these games competitive, and then master the art of winning them. For those who have been part of the journey – whether for one match or several – their Ryder Cup experiences will be right up there in the forefront of their minds and hearts.

With preparations well under way for 2008 in the US, there is plenty of evidence that the American giant is finally getting round to doing something positive to halt this long losing run: five defeats in the last six matches. Their captain Paul Azinger has asked for, and got, wholesale changes in the selection process; like Europe there is a year's qualification only, and just in case really good players slip through the net he has doubled his captain's picks to four. For the first time since 1999 he is using the prerogative of home advantage to restore foursomes as the morning format for the first couple of days, a form of the game Europe has not done so well at down the years. Those who have been predicting a loss of US interest in a competition that they seem unable to win could not be further from the truth. The Ryder Cup saga will run and run. Thank goodness!

ACKNOWLEDGMENTS

My thanks to Tony Jacklin, Bernard Gallacher, Sam Torrance, Bernhard Langer and Ian Woosnam for taking the time to revisit their experiences as Ryder Cup captains; to Colin Montgomerie for his insights into what it was like to play under the various captains of the teams of which he was a part, and for taking the time to write his introduction to this book. My thanks also to Renton Laidlaw for reading through the manuscript and correcting all the schoolboy errors that had inevitably crept in. Without their invaluable input, this book could not have been written.

INDEX